CIVILIZATIONS OF THE UNCONSCIOUS

OR

THE DECIPHERMENT OF
THE LINEAR A SCRIPT

BY NANDINI DICKENS

Hibiscus Press

Civilizations of the Unconscious or The Decipherment of the Linear A Script

By Nandini Dickens

Copyright © 2014 by Nandini Dickens. All rights reserved. No part of this book may be reproduced or transmitted in any form or by any means, electronic or mechanical, including photocopying, recording or by information storage and retrieval systems, without written permission from the author, except for brief excerpts in critical reviews and articles.

Published by Hibiscus Press. All inquiries should be addressed to Hibiscus Press, Address given at the website www. hibiscuspress.biz.

Book Design by Sensical Design & Communication

ISBN-13: 978-0-6159-2201-0
ISBN-10: 0615922015

Printed in the United States of America

TABLE OF CONTENTS

Я

Introduction	1

BACKGROUND TO THE LANGUAGES AND THEIR ASSOCIATED SCRIPTS   5

1. The Aegean Bronze Age and a Chronology of Ancient Crete   7
2. The Mycenaean Civilization   21
3. The Minoan Civilization of Crete   26
4. The Civilization of Ancient Lycia   55
5. Troy or Ilium   59
6. The Civilization of Ancient Cyprus   62
7. The Elamite Civilization   64
8. Connections Between The Civilizations Of Elam, The Indus Valley, And Central Asia   71
9. The Civilizations Of Ancient India   73

THE UNDERLYING LANGUAGES AND SCRIPTS   95

10. The Languages and Scripts of Ancient Lycia and Caria   98
11. The Language and Scripts of Ancient Elam   106

12. The Proto-Elamo-Dravidian, Proto-Dravidian, and Dravidian
    Languages   113
13. The Indus Script   117
14. The Scripts and Languages of Ancient Cyprus   122
15. The Decipherment of the Linear B Script   129
16. The Underlying Language of the Linear A Script   139
Conclusion: The Link Between Ancient Crete, Ancient Cyprus,
    Ancient Lycia, Ancient Elam, and The Indus Valley
    Civilization   177

Bibliography   186
Index   196

LIST OF MAPS

1.	The Bronze Age Civilizations of the Aegean	6
2.	The Tectonic Setting of the Volcanic Eruption of Thera 1625 B.C.	13
3.	The Dialects of Ancient Greece. 500 B.C.	15
4.	The Map of Bronze Age Crete	27
5.	The Map of Ancient Lycia, Ancient Cyprus, and Hittite Anatolia	54
6.	The Map of Ancient Elam, the Persian Plateau, and the Indus Valley	65
7.	The Map of the Indus Valley Civilization	74
8.	The Migrations of the Indo-Aryans	79
9.	The Hypothesized Migration of the Elamo-Dravidians	176

LIST OF CHARTS

1.	The Alphabets of Lycia and Caria	102
2.	The Indus Script	121
3.	The Cypriot Syllabary	127
4.	The Scripts of Ancient Crete	128
5.	The Linear B Symbols	134
6.	The Tamil Alphabet	144
7.	The Hypothesized Linear A Syllabary	146
8.	The Linear A symbols	154
9.	The Transaction Signs	160
10.	The Manning and Equipment of Ships	168

LIST OF ILLUSTRATIONS

1. Elements relating to the Chronology of the Aegean Bronze Age   17
2. Artifacts from the Shaft Graves of Mycenae and from Knossos   22
3. Architectural Elements of the Palace of Knossos   32
4. Minoan Vases   34
5. The Spectator Sport of Bull Leaping   36
6. Minoan Religion   39

ACKNOWLEDGMENTS

Editor: Brooke C. Stoddard

The following artwork and maps were done by Robert E. Pratt:
Cover Design
Plate 2. Gold Mask, Alabaster Vase, Lion Hunt Bronze Dagger, Steatite Rhyton, Silver Rhyton
Plate 3. Priest King Plaster Relief.
Maps 1–9

Juan-José Marcos. © Alphabetum Unicode, A font for ancient scripts. juanjmarcos@yahoo.es

The rest of the artwork not listed above are from The Palace of Minos at Knossos, Vols. I–IV. Evans, A.J. Public Domain.

Bull Leaping Fresco. File: Bull-leaping.jpg – Wikimedia Commons PD-US; PD-ART. Original uploader was Chris O at en.wikipedia (http://en.wikipedia.org) Public Domain.
http://commons.wikipedia.org/file:Bull-leaping.jpg

INTRODUCTION

THIS BOOK PROPOSES evidence for deciphering the Linear A incriptions of ancient Crete and demonstrates links that the Cretan civilization had to others of the same period.

In the quest for decipherment of this elusive script over the past century, researchers have scrutinized several language families and have even entertained the possibility that Linear A is a language isolate. Serious consideration has been given to two main language families, Indo-European and Semitic, because they were both spoken in the region of the Eastern Mediterranean around the 2nd Millennium B.C.

The Indo-European languages studied by scholars with respect to Linear A include Greek, Hittite, Luwian, Indic (Indo- European), and more recently Lycian. John Chadwick, who collaborated with Michael Ventris in discovering that Linear B was an archaic form of Greek, dismissed Greek as being the underlying language of Linear A. However, there does appear to be a link between Lycian and Linear A, a matter to be discussed in the ensuing chapters. There is no convincing evidence for the language of Linear A being related to the other three languages. Similarly none of the Semitic languages, including Akkadian, appear to be the underlying language of Linear A.

Unfortunately, relatively few Linear A tablets have survived the ravages of time. In part this is because of the occupation of Crete by the Mycenaean Greeks, who adapted Linear A to write their language in Linear B (before the final destruction of the Cretan palaces and administrative centers around 1200 B.C. much of the administration of the country was done by the Mycenaean Greeks using Linear B as their writing system). Many of the surviving Linear A tablets are in poor condition and only partially readable.

One language group not seriously researched as a foundation for Linear A is the Elamo-Dravidian family, perhaps because of its speakers' distance from Crete. Some specialists in the field separate Elamite and the Dravidian families into two separate groups. Others, however, stipulate a relationship between the two, postulating the families had a common origin. The chief proponent of this theory is Professor David McAlpin of the University of Pennsylvania. Evidence will be presented to show that the underlying language of Linear A is an Elamo-Dravidian language, and that it was spoken over a wide geographical area that ranged from Crete in the west to the Indus Valley civilization of the east.

This book is divided into two sections. The first deals with the background civilizations of the different affiliates of the underlying language of Linear A. No attempt has been made to make the discussion on these backgrounds comprehensive. Rather, certain relevant features supporting evidence for the language as a foundation for Linear A and showing links with other cultures speaking a similar language have been selected. The second section deals with the underlying language of Linear A and its links with associated languages.

INTRODUCTION

However, I have tried to make this book more than the decoding of Linear A, the civilizations it reveals, and the links between them. I have also tried to show the influence these cultures had on their surrounding ones as well as have had on present civilizations.

BACKGROUND TO THE LANGUAGES AND THEIR ASSOCIATED SCRIPTS

CIVILIZATIONS OF THE UNCONSCIOUS

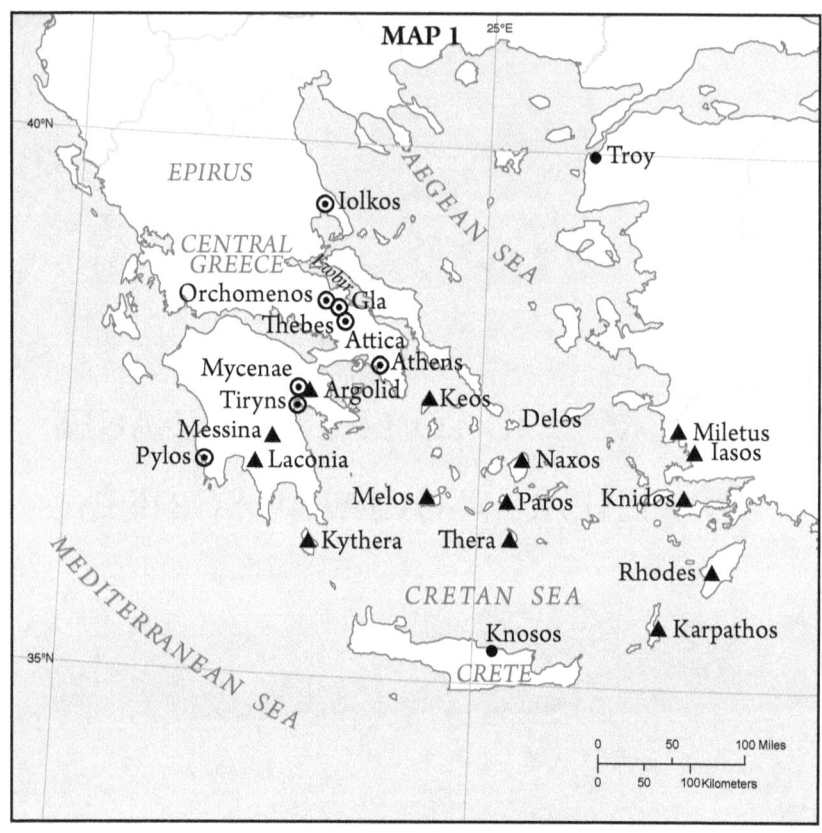

The Bronze Age Civilizations of the Aegean

⊙ Major Mycenaean Sites   ▲ Minoan Settlements or Areas of Influence

Iolkos	Melos	Rhodes
Mycenae	Paros	Miletus
Tiryns	Keos	Knidos
Orchomenos	Thera	Iasos
Gla	Naxos	Messina
Pylos	Kythera	Laconia
Thebes	Karpathos	Argolid
Athens		

CHAPTER ONE

THE AEGEAN BRONZE AGE AND A CHRONOLOGY OF ANCIENT CRETE

㭀

Bronze Age is the term used by archaeologists and historians for the period between 3500 and 1000 B.C. when bronze, an alloy of copper and tin, was the predominant metal used for weapons of war, toolmaking, industry, and artwork. The Bronze Age was predated by the Neolithic or New Stone Age, when copper, obsidian, and flint predominated. Following the disruption of trade routes for raw materials—primarily tin from Asia Minor and Cornwall—by the invasions of peoples from the north around 1200 B.C., iron began to be used as a replacement; thus was ushered in the Iron Age. The Bronze Age saw the earliest of the great civilizations of the Near East and the Eastern Mediterranean, including those of the Sumerian Kingdom of Mesopotamia, the Egyptian Old Kingdom, and the Minoan civilization of Crete.

The excavations of an amateur archaeologist revealed the Bronze Age civilization known as Mycenaean. Growing up in Mecklenburg, Germany, Heinrich Schliemann had been introduced to the works of Homer through his father, a lover of ancient history. Briefly, *The Iliad* tells the story of the ten-year siege of Troy, a city in Asia Minor, by the

Mycenaean Greeks. As told in the story, the conflict was precipitated by the abduction of Helen, queen of Sparta and wife of Menelaos, by the Trojan prince Paris. The Greek contingent was led by Agamemnon, king of Mycenae and the brother of Menelaos, while the Trojan contingent was led by Hector, the brother of Paris. The conclusion of the epic was the slaying of Hector by the Greek warrior Achilles, and the funeral rites held in his honor by the Trojans. The story continues in a second epic, *The Odyssey*, which relates the tribulations of an Agamemnon warrior, Odysseus, king of the Greek island of Ithaca, attempting to reach his home after the end of the Trojan war. Later Greek writings relate that the Greeks who fought in the Trojan war returned home to death and destruction and that their Mycenaean civilization collapsed.

The Greeks of the Classical Age believed in the historicity of Homer's *Iliad* and *Odyssey* and treated the poems with reverence. Later generations, however, read the poems as works of great literature rather than as factual history. By the 19th century A.D. there was no evidence of Troy or of most sites mentioned in the poems. Such identified sites as Mycenae and Tiryns were in ruins and showed little of the grandeur described by Homer. This scant archeological record together with the description in the epics of the active involvement of gods and other supernatural beings in the affairs of men had long bred skepticism. Schliemann, however, became obsessed with discovering the sites described in the *Iliad's* epic struggle. After years of hardship, he became a wealthy businessman, and taught himself several languages, including Greek. In 1876, using the epic poems together with other writings of the ancient Greeks and the works of Pausanias as a guide, he excavated the sites of Troy and Mycenae, making spectacular discoveries. As Mycenae was the most important of the Greek cities of the time, he termed the civilization Mycenaean. While some scholars acknowledge the presence of advanced Bronze Age civilizations in the areas of Mycenae and Troy, they express doubts on the historicity of the epic tales and view the characters as fictional. The consensus of the ancient Greek historians, however, was that the Trojan war took place around the end of the 13th century or early 12th century B.C.

Schliemann's discoveries led to the discovery of another Bronze Age civilization by another amateur archaeologist, Sir Arthur Evans, an antiquarian and the keeper of the Ashmolean Museum at Oxford. He hypothesized that the advanced civilizations of the Bronze Age cities of mainland Greece could not have functioned without the use of writing. His discovery of engraved sealstones on the Greek mainland, which were said to have originated in Crete, led him to excavate in Knossos, the ancient capital of Crete, in 1900. He fully expected to find another Mycenaean city. Instead he discovered the archaeological remains of a much older and more advanced civilization than that of the Mycenaeans. He called it Minoan after the legendary king of Crete according to ancient Greek writings. During his excavations of the Palace of Knossos, he discovered a cache of inscribed clay tablets with two different sets of writing. He termed them Linear writing of class A and Linear writing of class B, the former having being found at an archaeologically older level. The clay tablets had been sunbaked and were therefore perishable. They had, however, been preserved by the fires that had led to the final destruction of the palace around 1200 B.C. He termed the engraved sealstones that had been found mainly in eastern Crete "Hieroglyphic," because he thought they resembled Egyptian writing.

Before entering a discussion of the Mycenaean and Minoan civilizations, it is necessary to discuss three aspects.
1. Dating methods in archaeology
2. The historicity of the ancient Greek writings, including the histories and epics
3. The chronology of ancient Crete

1. SOME RELEVANT DATING METHODS IN ARCHAEOLOGY

(a) Absolute dating.

Absolute dating methods rely on using some physical property of an object to calculate its age. These include radiocarbon dating for organic materials, dendrochronology for trees and materials made of wood, and rehydroxylation dating for ceramic materials

(b) Relative methods.

Relative dating methods use associations built from the archaeological body of knowledge.

(c) Age equivalent Stratiographic markers.

These methods include: Paleomagnetism, which notes the Earth's polarity changes as stored in rocks; Tephrochronology, which gives the dates of volcanic eruptions; and Oxygen Isotope Chronostatiography, which records climatic changes, including those of the interglacial ages.

2. THE HISTORICITY OF THE ANCIENT GREEK WRITINGS

Historians have postulated a "Dark Age" for Greece between the destruction of the Mycenaean civilization around 1200 B.C. and the writing down of the Homeric epics around the 8th century B.C. During this time there was no evidence of an advanced civilization, or of literacy in the Greek world. It has been hypothesized that following the presumed Dorian invasion of the Peloponnese, the Mycenaeans fled to the highlands of Arcadia. Similarly it has been hypothesized that Mycenaean Greeks fleeing the Trojan war settled on the island of Cyprus, and possibly on Pamphylia on the coast of Asia Minor. Thus the Mycenaean dialect survived as the Arcadio-Cypriot subgroup of the Greek language in these two regions. In Cyprus a script called Cypro-Minoan, allied or derived from the Linear A script, was in use by the indigenous people. This script was thought to have been adapted by the Mycenaeans to write their dialect, which was in use from 1200 B.C. until about the 2nd century B.C, with the preservation of writings on stone. There is a high probability that writing occurred on perishable material as well. While the writings of the ancient Cretans, Linear A, survived as administrative texts on clay tablets, the curvilinear form of Linear A suggested that the script originated for use on papyrus or parchment rather than meant to be engraved on clay. There was widespread depiction of the papyrus plant either realistically or stylistically in art as shown in Chart 1 by both the Minoans and later by the Mycenaeans in frescos and on pottery at Knossos. Flat nodule sealings with the impression of seals on the upper end, and of scrolled up materials on the lower end are suggestive of the use of perishable materials. Further evidence was that inscriptions written in ink were preserved on two clay cups from Knossos, and that a serpentine sphinx from Hagia Triada with a hollow on its back appeared to be an inkwell analogous to those used in Mesopotamia. The major part of Cretan writings may have been written on perishable materials, including the leaves of the date palm, which grew in

Crete at that time. As did the surrounding cultures of the time, such an advanced civilization like that of Crete probably wrote histories, works of literature, contracts, treaties and letters of a personal nature. Because the Mycenaeans took over much of the culture of Crete, including its script, it is possible that they too wrote historical and literary works on perishable materials.

Regarding the historicity of the Homeric epics, archaeological and linguistic evidence exist supporting certain elements. Before Schliemann's excavations, there was no proof that either the Mycenaean civilization or the city of Troy existed. The ancient Greeks believed the Ionians had once lived on the Greek mainland but had fled due to invasions and had settled on the Aeolic islands and coast of Asia Minor; they also believed that Homer, the composer of the epics, had come from the Ionian coast. Not only are the epics composed mainly in the Ionian dialect with some Aeolic elements, but they also show a knowledge of the mainland.

Recent geological surveys done by Kraft and Luce compared the present geology of Troy with the landscapes and coastal features described in the *Iliad* and other classical sources, notably Strabo's *Geographica*. They concluded there was a regular consistency between Schliemann's Troy and the topography described in the epics, such as the locations of the Greek camps, the battles, and other geological features. In addition, excavations done at Mycenaean sites have revealed boar-tusk helmets and long shields, which are described in the epics although not used in later times.

That the Greeks of the Homeric age were aware of earlier writing is indicated in Book 7 of the *Iliad*, when Diomedes, who fought on the

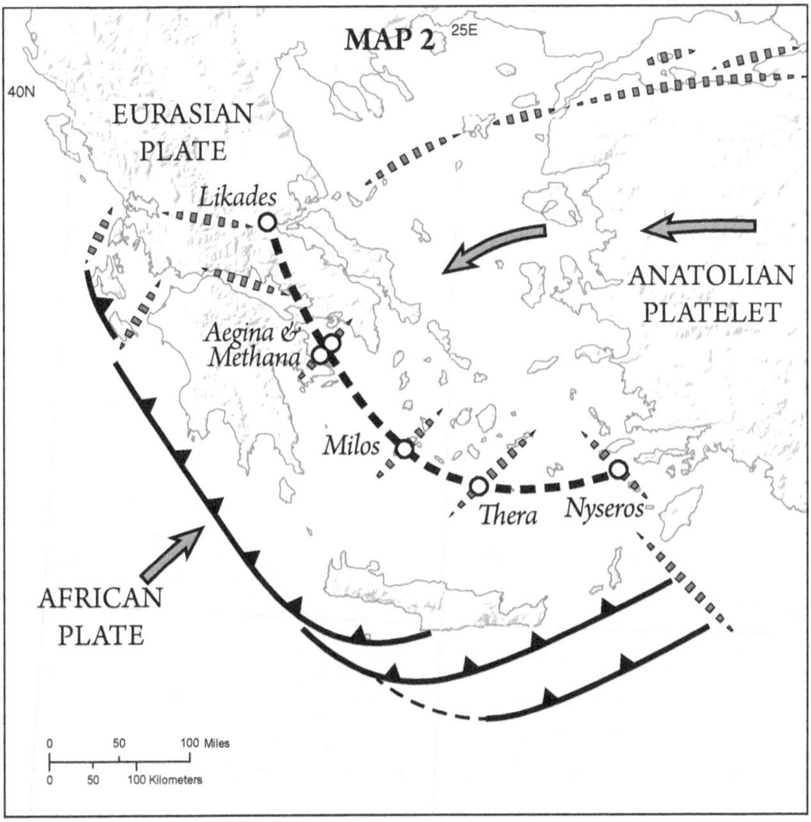

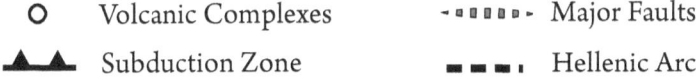

The Tectonic Setting of the Volcanic Eruption of Thera

| ○ | Volcanic Complexes | ▪▫▫▫▫▪ | Major Faults |
| ▲▲ | Subduction Zone | ▬ ▬ ▬ ▪ | Hellenic Arc |

side of the Greeks, asked Glaucus, who fought on the side of the Trojans, what his credentials were. In the course of his answer, Glaucus said that his grandfather Bellerphon had been sent to Lycia with lying letters of introduction, written in a folded tablet containing much ill will against the bearer. Bellerphon was from the Argives in the Peloponnese. The reference to the folded tablet indicates it was not written on clay but on another form of writing material, and that writing was used for purposes other than for administrative records.

Regarding ancient Greek myths and legends, they may, in spite of the overlay and distortions of time, have some truth to their core tales, especially when taken together with corroborative evidence. Overall it must be remembered that the Greek historians were much closer to the events described in terms of the time factor, and probably benefited from written documentation, as well as from oral transmission.

In conclusion it may be said that while there may have been a "Dark Age" on the Greek Mainland with the destruction of the Mycenaean sites together with their writings in Linear B, the fulcrum of Greek culture may have shifted to Cyprus and to the west coast of Asia Minor, with the survival of literacy.

3. THE CHRONOLOGY OF ANCIENT CRETE

Arthur Evans, the excavator of Crete, divided the Minoan period into three phases, and each of these into three sub-phases on the basis of pottery styles. These, however, do not coincide with the development of the other arts, with regional variation, or with decisive events in Cretan history. The Greek archaeologist Professor Platon proposed another system based on the building, destruction, and rebuilding of the palaces.

Evans' Classification		*Platon's Classification*	
Early Minoan	3000–2150 B.C.	Prepalatial	2600–1900 B.C.
Middle Minoan	2150–1600 B.C.	Protopalatial	1900–1700 B.C.
Late Minoan	1600–1170 B.C.	Neopalatial	1700–1425 B.C.
Sub Minoan	1100 B.C.	Postpalatial	1425–1170 B.C.

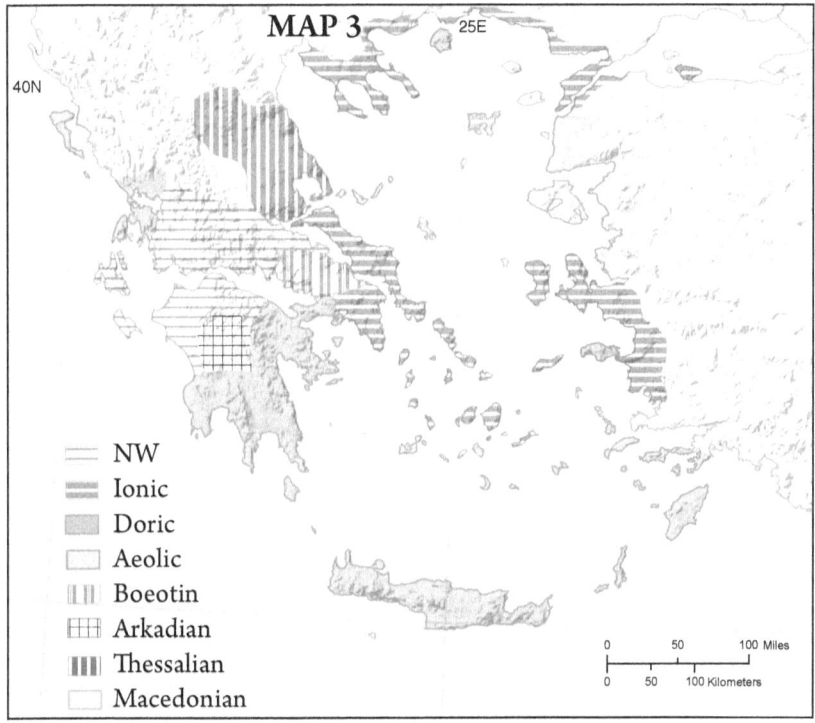

Dialects of Aegean Greece 500 B.C.

Both systems of classification need modification in the light of new archaeological discoveries, modern technologies of archaeological dating, and the corroborative evidence of the ancient Greek historians.

MODIFIED CHRONOLOGY

(a) Neolithic Period. 7000–3300 B.C.

The earliest settlers of Crete were a Neolithic people identified by their unique ceramic pottery. Around the beginning of the 3rd millennium B.C. evidence suggests a social upheaval with the arrival of new peoples having a distinctive style of pottery, the use of bronze, and a different culture.

(b) Early Minoan Prepalatial Period. 3300–2150 B.C.

This period was characterized by the type of settlements, architecture, artwork, pottery, and burial practices that included cist and tholos tombs.

(c) Middle Minoan Protopalatial Period. 2150–1625 B.C.

This was the period between the building of the first palace and the 1625 B.C. destructive volcanic explosion of the Aegean island of Thera and consequent fallout. The collision of the African plate with the Eurasian Plate together with the westward push of the Anatolian Platelet created a tectonically active region, with a string of volcanic islands forming the Hellenic Volcanic Arc. Thera was one of these islands. The exposed rocks of Thera's cliffs speak to several hundred thousand years of intermittent volcanic activity. During the Bronze Age a colossal volcanic explosion on the island was followed by a tsunami that affected the shores of central and eastern Crete, as well as those of mainland Greece, Asia Minor, and the Nile Delta. Studies show that when the tsunami reached Crete it was about nine meters high. Atmospheric percussion waves or shock waves caused fires. Ash fall would have destroyed agriculture and vegetation, leading to famine and disease. Dating of the explosion derives from the sulfuric acid content of ice cores, dendrochronology, and the paleomagnetism of pottery. Most specialists in the field place the eruption around the latter part of the 17th century. The eruption caused depopulation in eastern and to a lesser extent central Crete with a resulting diaspora and settlement of refugees in different parts of the Aegean. The legend of Atlantis, which originally came from Egyptian sources and was recorded centuries later by the Greek philosopher Plato, recounts the sinking of a highly evolved civilization under the

PLATE 1. Elements Relating to the Chronology of the Bronze Age Aegeam

Ruler of Crete
Middle Minien Period

Papyrus Sprays from
Frescoes and Pottery

Minoan Shorts worn by Archer
Prepalatial Period

sea. This could refer to the explosion of Thera. Scholars once believed Atlantis lay beyond "The Pillars of Hercules" and was therefore in the Atlantic Ocean. The name Atlantis, however, was derived from the mythical Greek god Atlas and not the Atlantic Ocean. Similarly 'The Pillars of Hercules," the name given by the Greeks to the Straits of Gibraltar could possibly be a misinterpretation for the entrance into the Mediterranean Sea through the straits of the Bosporus northeast of the Aegean islands.

(d) Late Minoan Neopalatial Period. 1625-1300 B.C.
Following the eruption of Thera and the destruction of the old palaces, new palaces were built on their sites. Around 1300 B.C. there was another destructive earthquake. Evans describes a seismic catastrophe with evidence of earthquake victims within the Pillar Crypt of the palace of Knossos, and of wholesale burials. This destruction was followed by the arrival of new peoples, and then about 100 years later, according to Evans, the final destruction of the palaces, which were not reoccupied. This final destruction is currently placed around 1200 B.C. Although the palace of Knossos survived, in the earlier destruction around 1300 B.C. some of the other palaces did not.

The dates accord well with the writings of Herodotus in his *History VII*, pages 170–171:

"Minos according to tradition went to Sicano or Sicily as it is now called, in search of Daedalus, and there perished by a violent death. Men of various nations now flocked to Crete which was stripped of its inhabitants. But none came in such numbers as the Hellenes. Three generations after the death of Minos, the Trojan war took place and the Cretans were not the least distinguished. But on this account when they came back from Troy, famine and pestilence fell upon them and destroyed both men and cattle. Crete was a second time stripped of its inhabitants, a remnant only being left, who form together with fresh settlers the third Cretan people by whom the island was inhabited."

The reference to "fresh settlers" and the "third Cretan People" appear to be the Dorian Greeks whose dialect became the main dialect of Crete. There is general agreement that the Trojan war took place either in the late 13th century B.C. or the early 12th century B.C. Three generations before the war would place the Mycenaean influx in the early part of the 13th century B.C. Thus Idomeneus, who according to the *Iliad* participated in the Trojan war, would have been the Mycenaean king of Crete. There is no evidence of violent intrusion, suggesting that the Mycenaean occupation of Crete was opportunistic and not one of military conquest.

(e) The Mycenaean Occupation of Crete. 1300-1200 B.C.
The Mycenaean presence is indicated by Mycenaean writings on Linear B tablets, Mycenaean pottery, caches of weaponry, militarism in their art and by Mycenaean burials. The Linear B tablets found at Mycenae, Thebes, and Pylos on mainland Greece have been dated to the end of the 13th century B.C. by the burnt destructive context in which they were found. There is growing consensus that the Linear B tablets found in Knossos can be attributed to a period roughly contemporary with those on the mainland. Supporting evidence for this is the recent discovery of a pair of tablets in Khania in Crete, in the burnt destructive context of the end of the 13th century. One of

these was written by a scribal hand already known at Knossos. The final seismic catastrophe that destroyed the palaces appears to have taken place around 1200 B.C. at about the same time as the Mycenaean sites on the mainland. Corroborative evidence also comes from the Oxford Philologist Professor Palmer, who had pointed out at an earlier time that there was a close resemblance in paleographic terms between the Linear B tablets at both Pylos and Knossos, and placed their destruction at about the same time period.

Therefore my proposed modified chronology would be roughly as follows. No attempt has been made to subdivide each of the periods, as these would be subject to modern methods of dating.

Proposed Modified Chronology

Neolithic Period	7000–3300 B.C.
Early Minoan Prepalatial Period	3300–2150 B.C.
Middle Minoan Protopalatial Period	2150–1625 B.C.
Late Minoan Neopalatial Period	1625–1300 B.C.
Mycenaean Occupation	1300–1200 B.C.
Doric Occupation	>1200 B.C.

CHAPTER TWO

THE MYCENAEAN CIVILIZATION

◁

MOST OF WHAT we know about the Mycenaean civilization comes from archaeological efforts in the region, plus information gathered from the Linear B tablets. This is supplemented by material gathered from the epic poems, as well as from Greek literature. The Mycenaeans were a Greek-speaking people who entered mainland Greece at the beginning of the 2nd millennium B.C. and founded a society lasting about 1600–1200 B.C., the last of the Bronze Age civilizations in the region. Mycenaean kingdoms emerged on the lower and cultivatable plains between mountain ranges. The chief kingdoms were those of Mycenae, Pylos, Thebes, Orchemenos, and Iolkos. Some of the palaces, including that of Mycenae, were built within heavily fortified citadels. Centralized authority as revealed by the Linear B tablets was in the personage of the king (Wanax), who collected taxes, redistributed goods, and defended the outlying villages. The palaces were the centers of industry, and slaves—mostly women and primarily from Asia Minor—formed an integral part of the economy.

It was within the citadel of Mycenae that Schliemann excavated the shaft graves that led to the discovery of the Mycenaean civilization. Unlike in prior centuries, rulers came to be buried in shaft graves with

CIVILIZATIONS OF THE UNCONSCIOUS

PLATE 2. Artifacts from the shaft graves of Mycenae and from Knossos

Gold Mask

Alabaster Vase

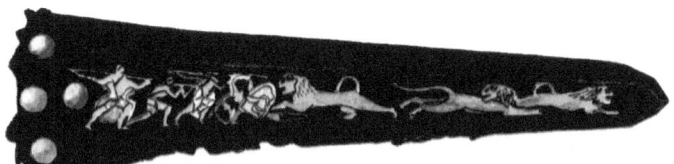
Lion Hunt Bronze Dagger

Steatite Rhyton Knossos

Silver replica of Rhyton-Shaft-grave Mycenae

a large amount of treasure. Shaft Grave A was excavated by Schliemann and the earlier Shaft Grave B by the Greek archaeologists Papademetriou and Mylonas. They are roughly dated 1600–1500 B.C. Within the graves, the faces of the men were covered with death masks of thin gold, and their chests were covered with gold breast plates. The women had clothes decked with gold discs and dress pins of precious metals, and they were accompanied by toilet boxes of gold. Children were wrapped in sheets of gold. Also within the graves were arrays of vessels of precious metals, swords, and daggers inlaid with scenes of hunting and nature, rings, engraved gems, bracelets, necklaces, and diadems. Many of the artifacts showed outstanding workmanship and a heavy Cretan influence. Linear A writing on a large bronze cauldron as well as Cretan symbols of bulls and double axes indicate that Cretans were the craftsman involved. The Minoan shorts worn in the hunting scene of lions on one of the shaft grave swords are shown on a Minoan seal in Plate 2. The famous gold Vapheio cups found in the burial tomb of a prince in Vapheio, near Sparta, have their counterparts in clay in Knossos. Within a few generations, burials began to occur in tholos, or beehive, tombs, suggesting dynastic changes and evolving organization. Certain wealthy families started building tholos or beehive tombs roughly in the period 1525–1275 B.C. Not only do these tombs resemble the tholos tombs on the Messara plain in Crete, but also one of the tholos tombs at Peristeria has two Cretan mason marks, namely a branch and two double axes cut into the facade to the left of the doorway. Two of the tholos tombs at Mycenae—"The Treasury of Atreus" and "The Tomb of Clytemnestra"—may have had their doorways imitated from the impressive north facade of the Cretan palace of Phaistos. The exterior facade of "The Treasury of Atreus" was faced with red and green marble. The capitals of the flanking columns of the doorways appear to be direct ancestors of the Doric style capitals of Classical Greece. The interior of the chamber vault was decorated with gilded bronze rosettes, a common decorative feature of Cretan art.

Archaeological work around the Mycenaean citadel investigating the shaft grave period has revealed no evidence of an advanced civilization and no elements of advanced architectural elements, nor even workshops for the shaft grave artifacts or their like. In fact, the finds of the shaft graves stand in stark contrast to the poverty of the Middle Helladic Period. A reasonable conclusion is that the artifacts were imported as finished objects, or made on demand by Minoan craftsman to suit mainland taste. One explanation for the discrepancy between the skilled workmanship of the artifacts in the shaft graves and the lack of similar artifacts in the region surrounding Mycenae is the volcanic explosion of Thera; likely this cataclysm stimulated a diaspora of skilled Cretan artisans to the island of Kythera and adjoining shores of the Peloponnese around 1625 B.C.

The Mycenaeans were a militaristic people, making overseas expeditions for booty and slaves. They were also constantly warring among themselves as chronicled in later Greek literature, specifically in "Seven against Thebes" and the Homeric epics. Asia Minor, Cyprus, and Crete were occupied in the final years before their demise. The final destruction of the Mycenaean sites has been attributed to different causes, including internecine warfare, natural disasters, invasions by foreign peoples or a combination of all three occurring toward the end of the 13th century B.C. In the case of Pylos, however, destruction appears to have been caused by an invasion from the north. Linear B tablet Tn 316 appears to have been hastily assembled, perhaps during the last hours of the palace. John Chadwick, who collaborated with Michael Ventris in the decipherment of the Linear B script, said it was a most disgraceful piece of handwriting, with frequent erasures and signs of illegibility, as though it was compiled in a great hurry. It spoke to the deployment of troops along the coast of Pylos, as well as of sacrifices to be made to the gods, of both gold objects and of human beings. While there is speculation about who the aggressors were, evidence points to the Dorian Greeks because the subsequent dialect of that area of the Peloponnese was Doric. It is hypothesized that the Dorians came from the area of Epirus where the Doric dialect was spoken as well. On a map of the early Greek dialects, the Dorian dialect forms an arc extending from Epirus through the southern Peloponnese, Crete, the Dodecanese and the southwestern coast of Asia Minor. As there is little evidence of skeletal remains in the coastal area of Pylos, it is likely that the Mycenaean population escaped to the highlands of Arcadia where was spoken an Arcadio-Cypriot dialect derived from the Mycenaean dialect.

CHAPTER THREE

THE MINOAN CIVILIZATION OF CRETE

Crete is an island in the eastern Mediterranean, strategically placed between the three continents of Africa, Asia, and Europe. Because of the subduction of the tectonic African Plate under the European Plate, the whole area has been subjected to volcanoes and earthquakes that have significantly contributed to the history and culture of Bronze Age Crete. Owing partly to its dominant position on the sea routes linking the Aegean with the Egyptian and Near Eastern world, Crete gave rise to a brilliant Bronze Age culture that lasted for about 2000 years.

Much of the information about Crete's Bronze Age culture comes from archaeological findings and from linguistic sources (Cretan hieroglyphics, Linear A, and Linear B scripts). Information can also be drawn from Egyptian paintings, Cretan artifacts in Egypt and Cyprus, and from settlements in the Aegean and the Levant. In addition, the writings of the Greek historians and authors provide a glimpse into Cretan society.

1. THE CHRONOLOGICAL PERIODS OF ANCIENT CRETE
(a) Early Minoan Prepalatial Period (3300–2150 B.C.)
The ancient Cretans may have emigrated to Crete from Asia Minor and the region of the Levant, around the middle of the 4th millennium

THE MINOAN CIVILIZATION OF CRETE

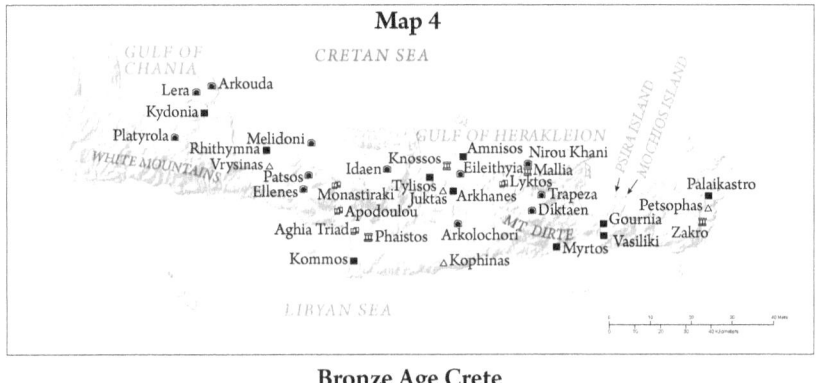

Bronze Age Crete

☷ Palaces	■ Settlements	⌂ Villas	◉ Sacred Caves	△ Peak Sanctuary
Knossos	Rhithymna	Aghia Triada	Melidoni	Vrysinas
Mallia	Kommos	Apodoulou	Patsos	Kophinas
Zakro	Tylissos	Monastiraki	Ellenes	Petsophas
Phaistos	Archanes	Lyktos	Idaen	Juktas
	Myrtos		Kamares	
	Gournia		Arkolochori	
	Vasiliki		Diktaen	
	Palaikastro		Lera	
	Arkhanes		Arkouda	
			Eileithyia	
			Nirou Khani	
			Trapeza	
			Idaean	

B.C. Before their emigration into Crete the island had been inhabited by a Neolithic people from about 7000 B.C. The transition from the Neolithic to the Bronze Age Cretans was marked by widespread dislocations and upheavals, together with radical changes in pottery. During this early Prepalatial period, settlements were in coastal areas such as Vasiliki, Mochlos, and Myrtos, where the inhabitants could engage in overseas trade. Archaeological evidence points to a decentralized culture with no hierarchical structures. The dead were buried in communal tholos tombs with corbeled vaults and that were used for centuries by entire villages. No evidence exits of exceptional dead. The societies appear to have been egalitarian in nature, without evidence of internal conflict or of military organization.

(b) The Middle Minoan Period of the Old Palaces (2150–1625 B.C.)

There are indications from around the early part of the 2nd millennium B.C. of migrations into central Greece and Asia Minor of Indo-European peoples and of resulting social upheavals. Perhaps as a response to these upheavals, a new political system was established in Crete, with authority concentrated around a central figure. Plate 1 shows the seal of what may have been such a figure wearing a crown, together with hieroglyphic writing. The first great palaces were built at Knossos, Phaistos, Mallia, and Kato Zakros. These became the centers of political, commercial and religious life of the island. They were destroyed by the eruption of the volcanic island of Thera around 1625 B.C. and new palaces were built over their sites using parts and foundations of the older palaces. At Phaistos, however, the west wing of the older palace was preserved, and the new palace was built at some distance from it. This together with archaeological excavations indicates that the older palaces were sophisticated in a construction and architectural intricacy which rivaled that of the newer palaces. The old palaces were characterized by a north-south orientation and by alignment with the surrounding topography. The palace of Knossos was aligned with Mount Juktas, and the palace of Phaistos with Mount Ida. In addition to the palaces, there were non-palatial complexes at Knossos, Mallia, and Archanes that had different forms, but similar functions. All the buildings had advanced drainage systems. The technical feats of this period are remarkable. Aqueducts such as the one at Knossos conveyed water from Mount Juktas via clay conduits passing over an arched bridge. The harbor installation at Pharos outside the Nile Delta with its quays and breakwaters is considered to be Minoan in construction. Built around 1800 B.C., it was able to accommodate 400 ships. The breakwater at Nirou Khani in Crete was built about this period as well. Road networks were set up with paved roads connecting not only the palaces but also the northern and southern shores. Minoan settlements appeared in Thera, Rodos, Melos, and Kythera. Trade was conducted by sailing vessels and sea-going galleys like those depicted on seal stones. Trading posts such as those at Phylokapi, Melos, and Kythera facilitated and safeguarded commercial dealings. In addition to the age-old cave sanctuaries, shrines were built on tops of mountains (peak sanctuaries) and in the palaces. The so-called Snake Goddesses date to this period. Burials were in Larnakes (sarcophagi), Pithoi (large jars), chamber tombs, and tholos tombs. Important pottery types are the exquisite Kamares egg-shell ware and the Vapheio type cups. Three different types of writing emerged during this period: Hieroglyphic, Linear A, and the Phaistos Disc. This period was a peaceful and prosperous time for the Minoans, who traded with Egypt, Cyprus, and the near East, including Syria.

(c) The Neopalatial Period (1625–1300 B.C.)

During this period, life in palatial Crete attained a level of artistic elegance and technical mastery that was seldom attained by the surrounding cultures. Built after the destruction of the older palaces, the new ones were huge architectural complexes with individual variations, but designed on a preconceived general plan. The main element was a central courtyard with multistoried constructions around it. The biggest and most complex of these, the one at Knossos, had over 200 rooms and was built on a timber framework supplemented with limestone and gypsum. The monumental gates of the many entrances

(Propylaea) were surrounded by stone friezes boasting rosettes, half rosettes, and spirals in relief. Light wells and windows endowed the architectural elements with movement and light. The west entrance was flanked by huge frescoes of bull leaping. On the west side were the ceremonial and state rooms as well as the cult rooms. Further west were the storage magazines with enormous clay jars (Pithoi), which held oil, wine, and foodstuffs. The east side held apartments and workshops. The latter included those of stone cutters, fresco painters, pottery makers, and scribes. The corridor of the draught board was named for the discovery there of a gaming board made from precious stones and metals. On the north side was a hypostyle banqueting hall. Outside the west side was the west court with huge "Horns of Consecration" and a theatre area. This may have been the area where bull leaping and other sports were held. The whole complex enjoyed advanced hydraulic and sanitation systems.

Overall the palaces appear to have been administrative centers rather than residential palaces. The so called "Royal Apartments" were too small to function as residences for the rulers, and the many entrances speak to people entering the many work areas to go about their daily business. The palaces appear to have functioned much like the Roman Agora, except that everything was concentrated in one enormous building. The rulers and important officials may have resided in one of the nearby so-called little palaces or villas. For example, the palace at Knossos was surrounded by "The Little Palace," "The Royal Villa," and "The House of The Frescoes," among others. The Palace of Phaistos had the nearby important villa of Hagia Triada. The organization of archives in most of these villas has yielded tablets with Linear A inscriptions and sealings, indicating that they operated in the same way as the palaces. Furthermore the confirmation that certain sealings in most centers originated from the same seal attests there was communication between centers and an exchange of produce and letters. There was a uniform economic and administrative system throughout Crete Although the Megaron of the palaces of the Mycenaean kings had little in common with the Cretan Palaces, building techniques such as the use of ashlar masonry, and multistoried construction, owe much to the Cretan constructions. The Megaron itself was copied from the Helladic predecessors of the Mycenaeans.

2. ARTISTIC AND TECHNOLOGICAL ELEMENTS OF CRETE
(a) Frescoes

Minoan frescoes were crafted using the "wet technique," that is, painting was done while the plaster was still wet. This required rapid execution, and as a result the frescoes show fluidity, dynamic motion, and a naturalistic style, which distinguish them from other Mediterranean cultures with their strict stylization and stereotypy. Frescoes could occupy the whole surface of a wall, be confined to small panels, or occur as long narrow friezes. The content of the frescoes appear to be both religious and secular. There were scenes of real life with animals, birds, and plants. A favorite plant was the papyrus, which was depicted both realistically and stylistically. There were huge bull leaping frescoes with both men and women dressed like men participating in the rituals. The attendant crowds attest to their being spectator sports. The frescoes from Akritori on Thera show portraits of everyday life and of town life. Scenes of hunting and warfare, so common in Mycenaean art, are absent.

PLATE 3. Architectural Elements of the Palace of Knossos

North Entrance of the
Palace of Knossos

Capital
Minoan Palm

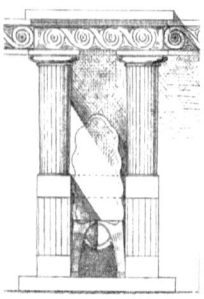

Throne and Canopy

Lamp Pedestal

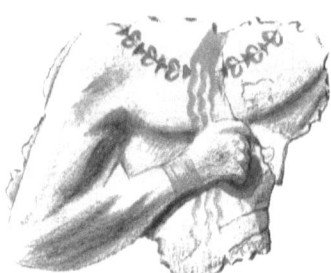

Priest King Plaster Relief

Stucco Relief of Griffins
Middle Minoan Period

(b) Sculpture and architectural elements

Large scale statues have not survived, probably on account of having been made of perishable materials such as wood. However, the life size plaster relief of the so called "Priest King" fresco from the palace of Knossos gives some indication of sophistication and realism, as does the head of a male figure in ivory (see Plate 3).

Columns with capitals can be inferred from the frescoes and stone pedestal lamps which are small versions of them. They foreshadow the Doric and Ionic orders of the capitals of later Greece. The fresco of the heraldic griffins flanking the throne in the throne room is thought by some to reflect Mycenaean taste when Mycenaeans occupied Knossos. However, a similar composition in painted stucco relief from the area of the East Hall dates to well before the Mycenaean occupation (see Plate 3).

(c) Pottery and vessels

The early Minoan Prepalatial Period is represented by Vasiliki ware; the Middle Minoan Protopalatial period is represented by the exquisite Kamares ware found primarily in the cave sanctuary of Mount Ida; and the late Minoan Neopalatial Period is represented by the Floral Style, which depicted various types of lilies, papyri, palms, and elaborate leaves, as well as by the Marine Style, which showed sea creatures like octopuses and fish against a background of rocks, seaweed, and sponges.

Before the entry of the Mycenaeans into Crete, both the Palace Style and the albastra attributed to Mycenaeans were evident in Crete, as shown in Plate 4. A painting from the tomb of Senmut, Egypt (15th

CIVILIZATIONS OF THE UNCONSCIOUS

PLATE 4. Minoan Vases

Faience Vases
Middle Minoan Period

Alabastron
Late Minoan Period

Vases of Late Minoan Period

Tomb of Senmut
Egypt 15th Century B.C.

century B.C.) shows Cretans carrying Palace Style jars. Such jars became much more evident after the Mycenaean occupation. The same can be said of the Close Style, where the depicted elements were already present in pre-Mycenaean Crete.

(d) Rhytons, or drinking vessels, in steatite

Rhytons, or drinking vessels, in steatite include one in the form of a bull's head that was replicated in the shaft graves of Mycenae with the addition of a rosette (Plate 2); the Chieftain's Cup, which depicts a coming of age rite; the Harvester Vase showing a harvest procession; the Boxer Rhyton showing boxing scenes; and the Sanctuary Rhyton depicting a peak sanctuary of the "Mistress of the Animals."

(e) Stone amphora

There is a similarity between an alabaster vase from Zakros and one shown in the shaft grave as seen in Plate 2.

(f) Metal work and jewelry

The Cretans created exquisite metalwork in gold, silver, and copper. They mastered the "lost wax technique," repousse (embossing), faience (granulation), niello, and the gilding of objects with gold foil. The Vapheio gold cups, with clay originals in Crete, show scenes of the capture of a bull. One scene shows the bull evading a net and throwing down one hunter while another hunter grasps the bull's horns to bring it down. A first impression was that one of the hunters with long flowing locks is a girl, but the figure's physiognomy is that of a male. The other two persons depicted also appear to have long hair. Evans describes the offering of hair to deities by young males. The capture of bulls and the offering of

PLATE 5. The Spectator Sport of Bull Leaping

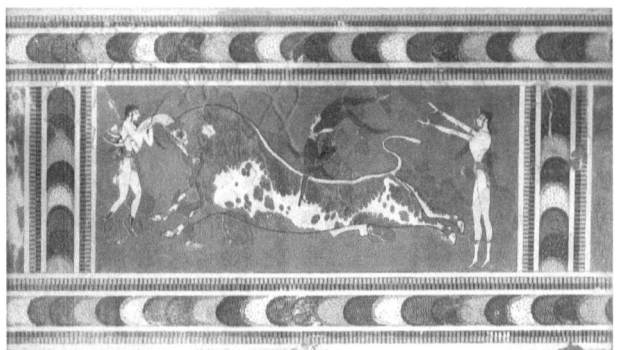

Bull Leaping Fresco

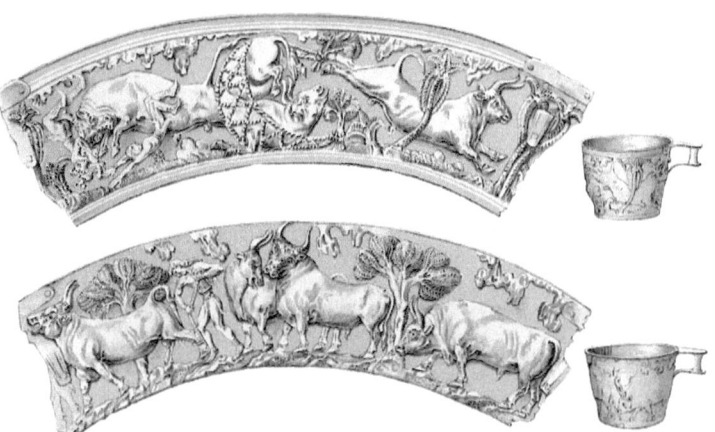

Vapheio Gold Cups Showing the Capture of Wild Bulls

Spectators at the Bull Leaping Rituals

hair to the deities may have been a "Rite de Passage" from adolescence to adulthood. Other scenes show the bull being finally lassoed (Plate 5).

In conclusion, I end with a quote by Evans on the Mycenaean occupation: "As compared with the great artistic tradition such as characterized the preceding palace stage that resulted from the great rebuilding, the new work takes a severely regulated shape. Lost is the free spirit that had given birth to the finely modeled forms of the athletes in the East Hall groups and the charging bull of the North Portico. Vanished is power of individual characterization and of instantaneous portraiture that we recognize in the lively miniature groups of the court ladies. Departed is the strong sympathy of wild nature still visible in the flowering plants and their rock setting as seen in the House of the Frescoes."

3. MINOAN RELIGION, RITUAL, AND CULTS

The religious nature of the Minoans is a complex subject that can only be inferred through the Linear A and Linear B tablets; the excavated artifacts of Crete; and the religious practices of ancient Crete and the Eastern Mediterranean, as well as through the mythology and religious practices of the later Greeks.

(a) Places of worship

(1) *Caves.* These were the most ancient places of worship. The Cave of Eileithiya is referred to in Homer's *Odyssey*, and the goddess herself will be discussed later. Others were the Kamares cave on the slopes of Mount Ida where the famous Kamares ware was found; the Idean Cave, also on the slopes of Mount Ida; the Diktean or Psychro cave on the foothills of Mount Dikte; and the Arkolochari cave near Galatos.

(2) Peak sanctuaries. Cult centers have been found near the tops of mountains. Those of Mount Juktas and Petsofa are two of the major ones. Artifacts included Kamares pottery, libation tables inscribed with Linear A, animal figurines, and replicas of body parts.

Both kinds of the above religious sites were found during the period of the first palaces.

(3) Domestic shrines. These include the Pillar Crypts, the Bench Sanctuaries, and the Lustral Basins.

(4) Outdoor shrines. These were walled enclosures with an altar and a tree.

Both domestic and outdoor shrines occurred during the Neopalatial period as did the use of caves.

(b) Cultic symbols

These included double axes with a purely symbolic function, Horns of Consecration, Baetyls or altars, sacrificial tables, Kernoi, snake tubes, bulls, agrimi goats, trees, birds, Minoan genii, and snakes.

(c) Representation of cult activities

These were depicted on seals, rings, mural paintings, sarcophagi, pottery, and figurines.

(d) Minoan deities and cultic symbols

Two objects of religious significance excavated from the period of the old palaces are the so-called "Snake Goddesses" and the "Dove Shrine Deposit," the former shown in Plate 6. The "Snake Goddesses" may have been priestesses. Snakes are important in regions ravaged by earthquakes. Anecdotally they give warning of impending earthquakes

PLATE 6. Minoan Religion

Paintings from the Hagia Triada Sarcophagus

Male Lyre Player
Hagia Triada Sarcophagus (L)
Palace (R)

Painting from the Hagia Triada Sarcophagus

Snake Goddess

Epiphany of the Goddess

Mistress and Master of animals

by emerging from the earth in large numbers, perhaps because being terrestrial creatures they feel the vibrations of the earth. In addition, the shedding of their skins symbolizes rebirth and regeneration. The "Dove Shrine Deposit" shows three pillars with capitals, together with beams on which three doves are sitting. Doves played an important part in Minoan belief. They appear to be the embodiment (epiphany) of a divinity, a representation of a goddess in bird form near her sacred places, a tree or a shrine. The doves can be interpreted as an emblem of the celestial power of the goddess as opposed to the snake, which reflected the goddess's underworld aspect and her earthly power. In the Elamite culture—discussed later—doves made of expensive materials were used as religious offerings. (The warrior goddess Athena of the later Greeks become militarized with a helmet and a shield but nonetheless was still associated with the owl and the snake, and the goddess of love, Aphrodite, was associated with the dove.)

After the destruction of the old palaces, most of the Peak Sanctuaries were abandoned and worship was concentrated in the palatial shrines of the new palaces. However, the caves and small outdoor shrines continued as places of worship. As shown on seals, the outdoor shrines had an enclosed altar and a small tree. In these places, a great female deity was worshipped with processions, ritual, music, and dance. There were no cult idols because belief in the epiphany of the goddess predominated. One of the aims of the ritual act was to have a vision of her. This was achieved with the help of ecstatic dances, music, prayer and mild-altering drugs. One such drug may have been opium, because there is a statuette of a poppy goddess. Religious life was characterized by mystic communion with the deity. Epiphany of the goddess had numerous representations in art and architecture. In the Isopata ring, a small figure is seen hovering in the air, and this may have been a vision seen to the worshippers or felt by them (Plate 6).

Bull leaping rituals came into prominence at this time. Rituals with the sacrifice of the bull, the symbol of the fecundity of nature, may have symbolized mastery over chthonic powers, important again in earthquake country. A mask of the bull was used in the rituals along with symbols associated with this animal, namely the double axe and the sacral horns, which were depicted in religious buildings and in works of art found in tombs and shrines.

Study of the representative arts shows the vast majority of characters who appear to be divinities were female. Male divinities are less evident; one was represented as being of a smaller size than female ones, and another was represented as master of the animals.

The Linear B tablets of the Mycenaean Greeks include 10 of the 12 gods of the pantheon of Classical Greece, Aphrodite and Hephaestus being excluded.

In Book Seven of his work, Greek historian of the 1st century B.C. Diodorus Siculus says, "The comrades of Minos buried the king with a shrine to Aphrodite. As their ships had been burned some of them established a city Minoa, while others established Engyum. They built a temple to the mothers. The cult of these goddesses, so men say, they moved from their home in Crete, since the Cretans hold these goddesses in special honor."

The word Potnia (Lady) was understood by the classical Greeks to be Demeter. She was attested in the pre-Hellenic cult of the Earth Mother in figurines and pictures of all kinds throughout the Bronze

Age. Potnia was the name given to her in the Mycenaean tablets. The word Demeter (Da-ma-ta) was also written in the Linear A tablets and will be discussed later.

The major gods of the Greek pantheon included Zeus, Hera, Artemis, Apollo, Athena, Demeter, Aphrodite, Dionysius, Poseidon, Hermes, Hephaestus, Hermes, and Ares. The deities of the underground were Hades and Persephone. If these cults had predated the breakup of the Indo-European people, they would have appeared in other Indo-European cultures. However, the only other name found elsewhere is Zeus. Chadwick, who collaborated with Ventris in the decipherment of Linear B and who had a specialized knowledge of linguistic change in ancient Greek, wrote that Zeus was the regular development of a form which could be restored as "Dyeus," and that the associations to his name show he was conceived of as the god of the clear sky. In the Vedas of Indian religious writing Zeus was known as Dayus Pitar, Pitar referring to father. Latin incorporated the word for father in their cognate of Zeus, Ju-piter. It can therefore be inferred that these new gods were borrowings from indigenous cultures.

As Crete had such an overwhelming influence on the Mycenaean civilization almost from Mycenaean civilization's inception—as evidenced by the artifacts in the shaft graves—it is probable there was borrowing in the religious sphere as well. There may also have been borrowings from the pre-Hellenic people of Greece, the Pelasgians, who may have exerted their influence in this sphere on the Greeks. A parallel example is seen in the case of the Hittites of Asia Minor who took over the religion of the indigenous Hatti as well as that of the neighboring Hurrians. Martin P. Nilsson in his book "The Minoan Mycenaean Religion" analyses this theme of acculturation. Pausanius, in his travels through ancient Greece, discusses their religious practices, which could be seen as borrowings from the surrounding cultures.

Following are discussions of selected aspects of Cretan religion and—through the Mycenaeans—its influence on the Classical Greeks.

Artemis

The Minoan goddess "Mistress of the Beasts," depicted on Cretan seals as the goddess of wild nature and associated with stags, lions, panthers, hares, griffins, swans, and other birds resembles the Greek goddess Artemis. "Mistress of the Beasts" was shown on mountain tops with rampant lions or walking with them by her side. And like Artemis she was associated with fertility and childbirth, being depicted with the tree cult and the sacred bough that conveyed life and fertility. She is the one supplicated to in the Linear A tablets. The Greeks referred to her as Eileithiya, and in the *Odyssey* Homer refers to the "Cave of Eileithiya" on the island of Crete.

In Greek mythology Artemis was associated with nature and the hunt as well as with fertility, childbirth, and the nurturance of the young. She was the principal deity for many Greeks of Asia Minor, and the temple dedicated to her at Ephesus was one of the "Seven Wonders of the World." Copies of the Ephesian Artemis show her associated with a large number of animals. Her best known title was "Potnia Theron," Lady of Wild Animals. She was also associated with the mountains of Crete and Arcadia.

Demeter and the Eleusian Mysteries

Demeter was the goddess of grain and vegetation, as opposed to Artemis, the goddess of persons and animals. The central myth of Demeter was that Hades, god of the underworld and death, abducted Demeter's daughter Persephone. Demeter searched the world for her, letting the fields go barren. Zeus intervened by allowing Persephone to remain with her mother for eight months of the year. The Eleusian mysteries of Classical Greece reenacted the story with dance and incantation at Eleusis, about 14 miles west of Athens and the chief center of the cult. At the climax of the secret nocturnal ceremony, the priest would hold up an ear of corn amidst reverential silence. The doctrine hoped that Demeter and Persephone would take care of initiates in the afterlife. The concept of Elysion, the happy afterlife, was seen as a Cretan concept, so contrary to the gloomy concept of Hades as detailed in the *Odyssey*.

Dionysius

Also known as Bacchus, Dionysius was the god of wine, vegetation, and religious possession. He was associated with the bull and the serpent, thereby indicating his Minoan roots. The Dionysian mystery cult was associated with the Orphic mysteries, Orpheus being regarded as the alter ego of Dionysius. Initiates of Orphism felt that they could commune with the god through spiritual ecstasy or intoxication. Orphism emphasized a belief in the transmigration of the soul with reincarnation being dependent on one's conduct in a prior life. Orphic devotees hoped for eventual release from cycles of reincarnation. An Orphic verse announced, "I have escaped from the wheel of pain."

Orphic tablets found near Sybaris and Rome, and at Eleutherna in Crete, exhort souls newly arrived in Hades to shun the spring of Lethe (Oblivion—souls drinking from Lethe would forget their lived lives and be reincarnated) but rather drink from the River Mnemosyne (Memory—souls would remember their lived lives and escape reincarnation), thus securing the end of transmigration and the attainment of higher consciousness.

These concepts of transmigration of the soul, karma, and reincarnation, appear again among the indigenous inhabitants of India, where they have played a crucial role in Indian and Southeast Asian religious life and are discussed in a later chapter.

Poseidon

Poseidon was the god of the sea and earthquakes, both unknown in the steppes of Eurasia, original home of the Indo-European people. Crete, an island surrounded by the sea and subject to catastrophic earthquakes, may have been the origin of this god.

4. FUNERARY AND BURIAL RITES

(1) Hagia Triada Discoveries

Four kilometers west of the palace of Phaistos are the ruins of a small Minoan palace named after the nearby village of Hagia Triada. The villa was built around 1600 B.C. and destroyed around 1300 B.C. by the first massive earthquake that ravaged Crete and led to the Mycenaean occupation.

This was where most of the Linear A tablets, as well as art treasures, were excavated by the Italian archaeologists Federico Halberr and Luisa Banti. Many of the art treasures were as impressive as those excavated at the palace of Knossos. They included frescoes of a naturalistic style and such famous steatite vases as the Harvester Vase, Boxer Rhyton, and Chieftain's Cup. During the period of occupation of the palace at Hagia Triada there was no evidence of Mycenaean occupation, including Linear B tablets, military equipment, or pottery types favored by the Mycenaeans. This is one of the reasons for the survival of a relatively large cache of Linear A tablets. In Knossos, where there was a Mycenaean presence, Linear B tablets predominated with very few Linear A tablets found. After the destruction of the palace of Hagia Triada, a Mycenaean type Megaron was built over its ruins.

About 150 meters northwest is a cemetery where the famous Hagia Triada sarcophagus was found. It is made of limestone and on the sides are painted representations of funeral scenes. On one of the long sides, two priestesses sacrifice a bull to the sounds of music played by a flute and a lyre. At one end of the other long side, a priestess is seen making a libation to the gods accompanied by the sacred symbols of the double axe, an altar, a tree, and a bowl of fruit. At the other end, three youths present a person with three gifts: a ship, presumably to travel to the "Isles of the Blessed," and two calves to serve as sustenance. The two smaller sides show women driving chariots drawn by agrimi goats and griffins. The sarcophagus representations are all purely Minoan. These include Minoan religious symbols, the sacrifice of the bull, Minoan dresses of the various religious officials, and Minoan musical instruments, none of which have representation at Mycenaean sites for this time period. Confirming the Minoan character of the sarcophagus, there is an almost exact representation of the lyre player on one of the Minoan frescoes at the Hagia Triada palace (see Plate 6). Also had there been a Greek presence, the chariots would have been pulled by horses, not agrimi goats. The sarcophagus is dated between 1370 and 1320 by modern methods of dating, and so was in use prior to the Mycenaean occupation.

5. HUMAN SACRIFICE

In 1981 two Greek archaeologists Yanis Sakellarakis and Efi Sapouna-Sakellaraki published the results of their excavations in Anemosophilia, close to the palace of Arkhanes and the nearby cemetery of Phoumi, alleging strong proof of human sacrifice by the Cretans. They described a structure, which they called a temple, with three rooms opening onto a corridor. The central room contained the charred feet of an idol, while the one to the east had bloodless offerings of agricultural products in pottery of a ceramic style that was an exact replica of those on the painted sarcophagus at Hagia Triada. In the west room on an altar was a skeleton of a youth of about 18 years old, 5'5" long, and in an extremely flexed position—legs tied behind him—with a bronze knife of about 16" long beside him. A skeleton lying near the altar was that of a powerful man 6' tall and in his late thirties. On the little finger of his left hand was a ring of silver and iron. There was evidence of building collapse, which Sakellarakis and Sakellaraki theorized was caused by the volcanic eruption of Thera, by their reckoning to have occurred about 1700 B.C. A skeleton in the corridor held the smashed remains of a Kamares type of pottery. Sakellarakis and Sakellaraki used the expertise of a criminologist and a physical anthropologist from Athens University to analyze the findings of the west room. They theorized that the youth was the sacrificial victim of the older man, and that he had been trussed up like a bull and drained of blood by having his carotid artery severed.

But difficulties and contradictions to this theory abound. Worked iron was not in use until around 1200 B.C. when trade routes for raw materials in the making of bronze were disrupted by invading people and the Mycenaeans turned to iron as the metal of choice. Additionally, the Cretans were a small people with an average height of 5'6". No evidence exists of burials of 6' Cretans before the entry of the Mycenaeans, whereas the shaft graves of Mycenae indicate burials of 6' men. The Hagia Triada sarcophagus has been dated between 1370 and1320 B.C., several centuries after the eruption of Thera, so that the vases which resembled those depicted in the sarcophagus in the temple would have to be re-dated. Additionally, in order to draw blood from a sacrificial victim, there is no need to truss the victim in an extremely flexed position. In fact, doing so would make it more difficult.

Although I do not think this is an instance of human sacrifice, strong evidence of human sacrifice does exist in the Linear B tablets of the Mycenaean Greeks. In Tn 316, the "Human Sacrifice" tablet, the word "Po-re-na" according to some scholars identifies human sacrificial victims, although other scholars believe they refer to sacristans, the bearers of the vessels. However, one of the lines under the heading of Pylos reads: Gold cup 1. woman 2. to B.... and X.... Two women are not needed to carry one gold cup. There are also instances of human sacrifices in the literary tradition. Agamemnon sacrificed his daughter Iphigenia in order to cause the winds to be favorable to the Greeks so that they could make the voyage to Troy.

Overall evidence points to any so-called "human sacrifice" occurring during the Mycenaean occupation of Crete. Under the circumstance, a reexamination by modern methods of dating is indicated, as well as work by a forensic anthropologist who would be able to determine the ancestry of the people involved, and especially if the 6' man was of Indo-European ancestry (Mycenaean).

Meanwhile I would like to put forward an alternate hypothesis. The so-called temple was rather a mortuary temple used for the preparation of the dead for burial, as the nearby cemetery of Phoumi might indicate. In addition, small bath-shaped sarcophagi were used for burial, which may account for the extreme flexed position of the youth. Because the Mycenaean Greeks buried their dead with weaponry, the bronze dagger might have been a burial item. The ceramics that were similar to those depicted on the Hagia Triada sarcophagus, points to them being funerary vases.

6. CANNIBALISM IN CRETE

Wall, Musgrave, and Warren discovered the skeletal remains of four children in the Late Minoan 1b period with cut marks on them, together with a Pithos with disarticulated phalanges and other "edible items." Two radiology experts said the x-rayed bones showed no evidence of pathology. Consequently, the researchers deemed the children to have been in normal health at the time of death and concluded the evidence pointed to cannibalism. Osteologists, however, are never able to estimate the time and cause of death with certainty. Because of the revised chronology of the Minoan Crete, I think the ceramic vessels, and the environs should be re-dated and the bones reexamined by a forensic anthropologist to ascertain the ancestry (Mycenaean or not) of the children. I think the evidence points to a secondary burial rite, as practiced by the Indo- Europeans, by which the skeleton is removed from its tomb, displayed to the relatives and then either returned to the chamber or mixed into an anonymous pile. In "A Mycenaean Second Burial Custom?" Dr. Cavanagh notes that in a few cases fire was used to clean the bones of flesh that had not decayed. In this case, the bones appear to have been cleaned by cutting the flesh away. Another Indo-European people, the Indo-Aryans, practiced a fractional burial rite, by which partial skeletal remains were first exposed to the elements and as a second step deposited in an urn.

7. MINOAN SETTLEMENTS AND REGIONS OF INFLUENCE

During the Neopalatial period, Cretan settlements, or areas of strong Cretan influence, became evident in the Cyclades, the Dodecanese, the western coast of Asia Minor, and the Peloponnese. In the Cyclades, Minoan influence is observed at the sites of Phylokapi on Melos, Peroika on Paros, Ayia Irini on Keos, and Akrotiri on Thera. In the Dodecanese, influence is evident at Trianda Ialysos in Rhodes, and at Karpathos and Kos. Settlements took place on the coast of Asia Minor at Miletus, Iasos, and Knidos. In the Peloponnese, there is strong evidence of a Minoan presence in Laconia, in the Argolid, and in Koryphasion, Peristeria and other sites.

8. THE RULERS OF CRETE

The seal of the ruler shown above and the building of the palaces in the form of administrative centers are evidence that during the Middle

Minoan Protopalatial Period Crete was ruled by a centralized authority. Most of the knowledge about the last Minoan Ruler, Minos, comes from the writings of the ancient Greek historians, Greek myths, and the Parian Marble. The latter was a Greek chronological table covering the years 1581 to 264 B.C. inscribed on marble stele found on the island of Paros. The name of the last ruler was most probably "Min" but it was given the typical Greek ending of "os," like Alexandros, by the Greeks. Min in Tamil means star or fish, and is discussed in greater detail in the section on the Indus Valley Civilization. According to the Parian Marble, there were two rulers with the name of Minos, the first king attaining kingship in 1506 B.C. and the other in the latter part of the 14th century. It appears to be a family name rather than a title like Pharaoh, because other Cretan kings are referred to by other names. The last Minos was said to have achieved naval supremacy in the Aegean by driving out pirates on the islands and placing his sons to govern them. He also had a reputation of being a great lawgiver. Every ninth year he would go to Knossos (implying that he lived elsewhere), commune with Zeus and promulgate the laws by which he would govern Crete. Every eight years the full moon falls on the equinoxes, and this may be the reason for the ninth year to be chosen. (The Indus Valley Civilization used a base-eight numerical system, which is very rare, and will be discussed later.) Lycurgus (8th century B.C.), the legendary law giver of Sparta, studied the forms of government in Crete and in Ionia on the west coast of Asia Minor, which included the ancient settlements of the Minoans -- Iasos and Miletus -- before promulgating his laws. Lycurgus, in fact, is depicted on several U.S. buildings, including the chamber of the U.S. House of Representatives in the United States

Capitol, because of his legacy as a lawmaker.

The central Greek myth regarding Minos is as follows: Androgeus, the son of Minos, was killed by jealous Athenians after he had won all the events at the Pan Athenian Games. In revenge Minos decimated the Athenian countryside, and was able to extract from the Athenians a treaty whereby they would send seven youths and seven maidens every ninth year to Crete (corresponding to the lunar alignments). According to the Parian Marble, the first of these tributes occurred in 1295 B.C. Two Greek traditions exist about the fate of the youngsters. In one, they were offered as a sacrifice to the Minotaur (Mino-Taurus), half-bull half-man, who was the offspring of the passion of Pasiphae, the wife of Minos, for a bull. In the other, the youths were given to the victors of funeral games as slaves. It appears that the funeral games depicted in the *Iliad* had their origin in Crete. When the third contingent of Athenian youths arrived in Crete with Theseus—the son of the Athenian King—Daidolos, an inventor and craftsman in the court of Minos and Ariadne, the daughter of Minos, were instrumental in allowing Theseus to kill the Minotaur and escape together with the rest of the contingent. Minos and a contingent of Cretans pursued Daidolos to Sicily where Minos was murdered by Cocalus, the king of Agrigentum. As the ships of Minos' followers had been burnt, the Minoans founded and settled in the cities of Minoa and Engyum. The Parian Marble would place the arrival of the third contingent of youths arriving in Crete at around 1277 B.C., three generations before the Trojan war as described by Herodotus. If a generation is about 22 years, the war would have occurred 66 years later, in 1211 B.C. and the fall of Troy in 1201 B.C. The Parian Marble places the fall of Troy in 1209 B.C. After the ten-year war, the returning

Mycenaeans were met with a catastrophic event that wrecked their palaces, leading at first to famine and disease and later an occupation of the island of Crete by the Dorians. As discussed earlier, following the death of Minos and the depopulation of Crete, different peoples flocked to the island, first the Mycenaeans in large numbers and later the Dorians.

9. THE PEOPLES OF CRETE AFTER THE DORIAN OCCUPATION.

Homer, *Odyssey* 19, lines 172–177: "There is a land called Crete. . . . Language with language is mingled together. There are Akhaians, there are great hearted Eteocretans, there are Kydones and Dorians in their three clans, and noble Pelasgians."

Of these, the Achaeans and the Dorians are Greeks. Ancient tradition linked the Pelasgians with the Etruscans, Tyrrhenians and Lydians. The Kydones, who occupied modern day Khania, could possibly be the remnants of the Minoan population, while the Eteocretans could be the original Neolithic population of Crete.

Ancient Lycia, Ancient Cyprus, and Hittite Anatolia
    Troy (Wilusa)
    Arzawa (Luwians)
    Miletus (Millawanda)
    Lycia (Lukka)
    Cyprus (Alashiya)

CHAPTER FOUR

THE CIVILIZATION OF ANCIENT LYCIA

THE LYCIANS WERE one of the ancient peoples of Anatolia who inhabited the area between the bays of Antalya and Fethiya. Herodotus wrote that according to Greek tradition the Lycians originally came from Crete after a dynastic struggle between Minos and his brother Sarpenden, with Minos prevailing. According to the historian Ephorus, Sarpenden and his followers appeared to have first crossed to Caria where they founded the city of Miletus, naming it after the Cretan city of the same name. Another tradition held that the city of Idrias further south in Caria was the first city founded by the settlers. Their final destination was Milyas just to the southeast on the coast, a region later called Lycia, where they displaced the tribe of the Solymi.

Herodotus also recorded that the customs of the Lycians were partly Cretan and partly Carian, which gives credence to the assertion that their original home was Crete, as well as to the migratory route taken by them. They called themselves Termilae and their country Termmissa. These were the names by which they referred to themselves and to their country, and by which they were referred to by their neighbors for centuries afterwards. The name Lycia may have come from Lycus, son of Athenian king Pandion, who was expelled by his brother Aegeus and who joined Sarpenden with his own followers. According to the Parian Marble, Aegeus reigned in Athens in 1295 B.C. In Chapter Three we saw that Minos ascended the throne in the latter part of the 14th century, and this points to the time when the Termilae founded their cities in Anatolia. Thus the time-frame accords well with the traditions for the entry of the Lycians and the Athenian Greeks into Ancient Lycia. There is a close resemblance between the word Termilae and Tamils.

The earliest historical references to Lycia date to the late Bronze Age. Numerous Egyptian, Hittite, and Ugaritic texts refer to the Lycians as Lukka. In Lycia, the Greek inscriptions of the 5th century B.C. refer to themselves as Lycians, while the Cretan inscriptions refer to themselves as Termilae.

The Lycians were a fiercely independent people who resisted all attempts at domination. They were the last peoples in Asia Minor to be incorporated into the Roman Empire. The first recorded instance of Lycian resistance occurred in 540 B.C. when the Persians attacked the Lycian capital of Xanthus. The Lycians put up a heroic fight and chose mass suicide over surrender. Later they were caught in the struggles between the Greeks and the Persians. In 362 B.C. after an unsuccessful satrap revolt they came under the control of a Persian satrap of Carian descent. The Carian rulers began suppressing the indigenous culture of Lycia and imposing Helleno-Carian culture upon it. For example, the Letoon triangle, a trilingual stele which was instrumental in deciphering the Lycian language, discusses the introduction of two Carian cults.

The "Democratic Lycian Federation," the first known democratic union, was envied and extensively studied by Classical Greek writers. The Classical Greek writers envied the Lycians for the fact that whereas the Lycians enjoyed peace among themselves as a result of their federal constitution, the Greek city states were constantly at war with each other. The later Lycian league of the 3rd century B.C. was famous for its tradition of independent city states that had joined together to form a model political organization. No precise information on its early beginnings exists, but even under the dynasts of the 4th century B.C. Lycian inscriptions refer many times to the payment of fines to the "Federal Treasurer of the Trmmili." This phrasing points to the Cretan rather than the Greek origin of the Lycian Federation. The federal coinage of the cities that participated in the league was marked by a distinctive symbol, the Triskele.

Strabo, Livy, and Pliny supplied information about the later league. Twenty-two member states elected one to three representatives to the assembly (Synedrion) depending on the size of the city. Taxes and other financial burdens were allocated proportionately. Each year when the Assembly convened, it elected the Lysarch and other federal officers. A league court and judges settled disputes between cities, and minor magistrates and jurors elected by each city settled issues in the federal courts. The league held extensive rights over the cities of Lycia and controlled communal land, trade rights, and the rights of citizens to marry. The federation met at Patara, where the parliament building contains rows of seats arranged in a semicircle similar to the seating arrangement adopted by the U.S. Congress; it remains a tourist attraction to this day.

The men who framed the American constitution studied the Lycian federal system of government and its proportional representation as a model for their own government. The Federalist papers, essays written between 1787 to 1788 urging New Yorkers to ratify the proposed constitution, comprise two—Numbers 9 and 16 by Alexander Hamilton about the Union as a safeguard against domestic faction and insurrection -- mentioning Lycia as a template. Federalist Paper Number 45 written by James Madison about the alleged danger from the powers of the Union to the state governments also takes up the good example of the Lycian confederacy.

Ancient writers said that the Lycians had customs of their own, a style of unique funerary architecture, and a language of their own written in characters peculiar to them. Possibly they were using the Linear A script. Herodotus also wrote about one of their customs, which he described as peculiar to them and unique to mankind. He wrote that the Lycians reckoned their lineage not by their father's side, but by their mother's. Moreover, the children of a female citizen, even from a slave, were legitimate, whereas those of a male citizen from a foreigner or a concubine were illegitimate.

Among the Lycians, the goddess Leto and her children Apollo and Artemis were worshipped, together with an earlier goddess thought to be an ancient mother goddess Eni Mahanahi. Artemis had a magnificent temple at Myra, and was referred to as Artemis Eleuthera, reminiscent of Eileithiya, the Cretan goddess.

Because of the links between Crete and Lycia it can be inferred that Crete probably had some sort of a federated system, as well as a matriarchal and matrilineal system.

CHAPTER FIVE

TROY OR ILIUM

CELEBRATED IN THE *Iliad* and the *Odyssey* of Homer is the city we know in English as Troy or Ilium. Hittites knew it as Wilusa, Greeks as Ilion, and Romans as Ilium. Believed mythical for centuries, it was very much real. Its ruins are located in northwest Anatolia, beside Mount Ida and slightly southeast of the Dardanelles, which the city guarded. Archaeologically the ruins are divided into nine levels or layers.

TROY 1-4

The first city on the site was founded upon a promontory in the 3rd millennium B.C. Troy 1 and 2 date from 3000–2250 B.C. Heinrich Schliemann and Carl Blegan found large caches of gold and silver plus tools and vessels of bronze and copper in the burnt destruction of Level 2. Every house that had been exposed had been deserted in great haste as fire swept through the settlement. Large quantities of gold ornaments and jewelry, and gold, copper, and bronze vessels as well as bronze weapons attest to the high degree of wealth and prosperity of the city's inhabitants.

TROY 5

Troy 5 corresponds to the entry of the Indo-Europeans into the area around 1800 B.C.

TROY 7A

Troy 7a corresponds to the period 1300–1190 B.C., the likely period of what we call the Trojan war.

The link between Troy and Crete is tenuous and seen mostly in the jewelry excavated by Schliemann in Levels 1–4 before the arrival of the Indo-Europeans. Unfortunately no evidence of writing of the pre-European Trojans has yet been found. But overall only a small part of Troy has been excavated.

As early as 2500 B.C. Minoan craftsman working in Troy fashioned earrings and bracelets of a fairly standard type. Typically, thin coils and chains of linked and plated gold wire and thin gold foil fashioned into petals and rosettes were widely produced. Stamping, enameling, granulation, and filigree were common. The gold jewelry can be compared to the destruction deposits found at Polochni on the island of Lemnos and to pieces from the tombs of Mochlos in Crete. A gold sauceboat and two-handled cups found at Kastri on the island of Kythera show Trojan influence, and Kastri may have been settled by refugees from the disaster that destroyed Troy 2. The hoard discovered by Schliemann and identified by him as the treasures of Priam and Helen predate the Trojan war by several centuries, even dated as noted to before the entry of the Indo-Europeans.

As to the language spoken by the Indo-European Trojans, there appears to be some evidence that it might have been a dialect of Greek.

Ventris and Chadwick, who collaborated on the decipherment of Linear B, show that over 58 names in the Linear B tablets are paralleled in the Homeric epics, of which 20 are Trojan names including that of Hector, the Trojan hero. In 1280 B.C. there was a treaty between the Hittite king Muwatalli and King Alaksandu of Wilusa. In the *Iliad* another name for Paris was Alexandros, which is a Greek name. It is true that in 1995 a biconvex bronze seal of the Late Bronze Age with Luwian writing was excavated. However, this has so far been a single artifact and thus does not prove Luwain was the language of the Trojans. Overall the inscriptions of the names on the Linear B tablets are another indication that during the so-called "Dark Age" a continuity of cultural information existed from the Mycenaean period to the Homeric age.

My final thought on Ilium is that it bears a close resemblance to Elam, to be discussed later.

CHAPTER SIX

THE CIVILIZATION OF ANCIENT CYPRUS

From the 6th millennium B.C. onwards Cyprus was settled by Neolithic peoples, who fashioned distinctive pottery and small figurines of what appear to be fertility goddesses. During the transition from the Stone Age to the Bronze Age, the settlers moved from the coastal areas to the great plain fronting the foothills of the mountains. The discovery of copper around 3000 B.C. made Cyprus an important trading center for the raw material needed in the making of bronze. The name Cyprus itself derives from the word for copper. Cuneiform records from Mari dating to the 18th or 19th century B.C. record copper from "Alashiya," the Bronze Age name for Cyprus.

It appears from documentary evidence, chiefly in the form of Egyptian hieroglyphics and cuneiform writings, that Alashiya, with a polyglot population of Hurrians, Semites, Hittites, and Egyptians, was more closely associated with the Levant than with the Aegean cultures. However, there appears to have been a trading settlement of Minoans on the island, by evidence of the use of a script called Cypro-Minoan, from the 16th to the 11th century, and which appears to be related to

Linear A. Toward the end of the Trojan war, from about the end of the 12th century, large numbers of Mycenaean Greeks entered Cyprus, making the Arcadio-Cypriot dialect of Mycenaean the language of Cyprus at that time. It is thought that the Mycenaean Greeks may have adapted the Cypro-Minoan script to write their language in the form of the Cypriot Syllabary. The Cypriot Syllabary appears to be related to three scripts: those of Cypro-Minoan, Linear A, and Linear B.

Because of the strategic position of Cyprus in the Eastern Mediterranean and of its deposits of copper, the island was subjected to successive settlements and conquests by different people. From 800 B.C., following settlement by Phoenicians, Cyprus fell successively to the Assyrians, the Egyptians, the Persians, the Macedonian Greeks, the Egyptians again, and finally to the Romans in 55 B.C.

CHAPTER SEVEN

THE ELAMITE CIVILIZATION

SCHOLARS DEBATE THE geographical and political extent of Elam. A Neo-Assyrian representation of Sargon's conquest (2300 B.C.) considers Elam to have encompassed the entire Persian Plateau. Elamite cultural influence extended farther still, reaching Central Asia, the present-day territories of Afghanistan, Pakistan, and the southern shores of the Persian Gulf. By the middle of the 1st millennium B.C., however, Elam's history was confined to Khuzestan at the head of the Persian Gulf and the adjoining mountains. The supposed eastern extent of the Elamite language area rests on the hypothesis that Elamite is related to the Dravidian language family, to be discussed in the Language section.

The name of the country of Elam is reflected in Sumerian as Elama, in Akkadian as Elamtu, and in Hebrew as Elam. For the Sumerians and the Akkadians, Elam refers to highland. The Elamites themselves referred to their country as Haltamti. In the Elamite language Hal refers to land or town. I contend that Tam refers to the Tamils. Controversy surrounds what Ti refers to. My belief is that overall the name refers to the "Land of the Tamils."

THE ELAMITE CIVILIZATION

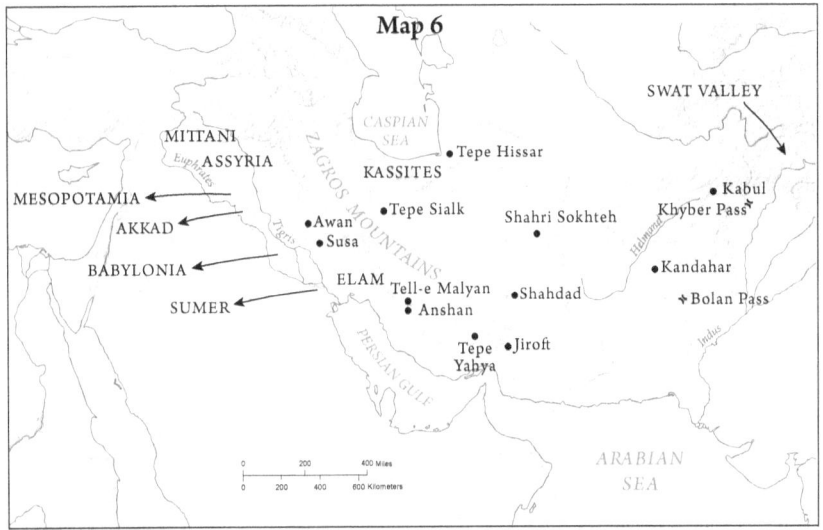

Ancient Elam, The Persian Plateau, and The Indus Valley

Owing to a scarcity of indigenous sources, the known history of Elam is fragmentary. Reconstruction is done through Mesopotamian documentation. Unfortunately for Elam, Mesopotamia coveted the timber, metals, and precious stones of the Persian Plateau, unreachable except through Elam. The documentation reveals endless strife not only of the Mesopotamian people amongst themselves, but also against the Elamites.

Conventionally the Elamite historical and language periods are divided as follows:

1. Proto-Elamite (3200–2700 B.C.)
2. Old Elamite (2700–1500 B.C.)
3. Middle Elamite (1500–1100 B.C.)
4. Neo-Elamite (1100–539 B.C.)
5. Achaemenid (539–331 B.C.)

1. THE PROTO-ELAMITE PERIOD (3200–2700 B. C.)

Proto-Elamite is the term used to designate the art and culture of the late 4th and early 3rd millennia. The Proto-Elamite script is the writing system found in sites stretching across the Persian Plateau. The controversy over whether the script represented the Elamite language is discussed in the Language section. Three of the Proto-Elamite states—Anshan, Awan, and Shimaski—merged to form a federation, as indicated by the titles of the kings and of the lines of royal succession. Elamite strength was based on its federated government structure that permitted maximum interchange of the natural resources unique to each region. The state of Susa, culturally Proto-Elamite, periodically was the jurisdiction of the Mesopotamian and Elamite states.

Mesopotamian documentation reveals that the Elamites had been a vassal state of Sumeria, but also in turn had subjugated Sumeria during this period.

2. OLD ELAMITE PERIOD (2700–1500 B.C.)

The Old Elamite Period was a time characterized by conflict, interspersed with periods of diplomacy between Elam and with the city states of Mesopotamia, as well as with those of Akkad and Babylon. The Akkadians attempted to impose their language and script on the Elamites. A significant event was the treaty between Naram-Sin (2291–2255 B.C.), the king of Agade in Akkad, and his vassal, King Khita of Awan in Elam. Its importance lies in many areas including the fact that the treaty was written in a simplified cuneiform script of the Elamite language. In the treaty, following an invocation to the gods, the Elamite king asserts "Naram-Sin's enemy is my enemy; Naram-Sin's friend is my friend."

Another important historical figure of the time is the ruler Kutik-In-Shushinak. He left a large number of inscriptions, not only in the Akkadian language and script, but also in the so-called "Linear script" in the Elamite language. The latter was a linear syllabic script used for a very short time during the man's rule from 2250 B.C. to 2220 B.C.

During this period there were two foreign invasions from the mountainous regions of the north, one by the Guti and one by the Kassites.

3. MIDDLE ELAMITE PERIOD (1500–1100 B.C.)

In 1210 B.C., King Shutruk Nahunte drove out the Kassites from Babylon. In 1200 B.C. he raided Akkad, Babylon, and Eshnunna, and carried home to Susa the Stelae of Hammurabi and of Naram-Sin, the statue and Obelisk of Manitushu, and the statue of Marduk. In 1120 B.C. the Babylonian King Nebuchadnezzar sacked Susa and Elam and returned the statue of Marduk to its home. It was at this period that the system of federation, distribution of power, and royal succession of the Old Elamite period broke down.

4. NEO-ELAMITE PERIOD (1100–539 B.C.)

The slow progression of the Medes and the Persians pushed the Elamites in the region of Anshan toward Susiana, which had been the second center of Elamite civilization for about a millennium and a half. The country of Anshan became Persia proper, while Susiana then and only then became known as Elam. The earlier Neo-Elamite kings had called themselves kings of Anshan and Susa.

The "Distant Medes" were designated by the Achaemenids as Parthians, Sagartians, Margians, Bactrians, Sogdians, and Arians. It can be noted that of all the Indo-European tribes only one called themselves Arian, to be discussed later. In spite of an alliance of the Elamites with their old enemy Babylon, in 637 B.C. Ashurbanipal of Assyria destroyed Susa, pulling down buildings and sowing the land with salt.

5. THE ACHAEMENID PERIOD (539–331 B.C.)

Under the Achaemenids the region administered from Susa became the province of Susa. Darius and his successors built palace complexes at Susa, which became the political center of the imperial court. Elamite was the first language used for formal inscriptions. The famous inscription of Behistan, written in Elamite, Aramaic, and old Persian, led to the decipherment of the cuneiform script by Rawlinson.

THE FEDERATED STATES OF ELAM AND MATRILINEAL SUCCESSION

The Elamite federated governmental structure was related to the culture's system of inheritance and power distribution. In later times the king lived in the federal capital Susa. His brother closest in age was viceroy and had his seat of government in the native city of the currently ruling dynasty; he was also heir presumptive to the king. A third official, the regent or Prince of Susa, was usually the king's nephew through his sister, or his son if there was no maternal nephew, and who shared power with the other two. On the death of the king, his brother the viceroy became king and the next brother became the viceroy. When all the brothers had died, the regent became the king. An example is that of one of the best known kings of Shimaski, Idadu the First. Precise dates are unknown but probably around 2000 B.C., a sister's son succeeded his uncle through the female line. Another example is that of Shilkhakha (between 1850 and 1830 B.C.), who shared power with his sister, and whose descendants claimed their legitimacy through her. In the later kings list she is referred to as "Sister of Shilkhakha." Francois Vallat has a different interpretation of the expression "Son of the sister of Shilkhakha" from other researchers in the field. He claims that it referred to royal incest and to primogeniture.

Corroborative evidence for matrilineal succession comes from a letter written by a king of Anshan and Susa, possibly Shutruk Nakhunte, who wrote to the Kassite king of Babylon (1182–1172 B.C.) laying claim to the throne because he had married the eldest daughter of the Kassite king.

Women had a prominent position in Elamite society. They ruled, conducted business, inherited and willed their property and were agents of succession. The matriarchal characteristics of Elamite culture survived up to the Neo-Elamite era when it gave way to the patriarchal system of its neighbors.

Information about Elamite religion comes not only from the treaty of Naram-Sin, but also from the building inscriptions of kings, and from consecration texts. It is difficult to disentangle which divinities were originally Elamite and which were Mesopotamian. The earliest document, the treaty of Naram-Sin (2280 B.C.), lists almost all the divinities who composed the Elamite pantheon at the time of the fall of the kingdom to Ashurbanipal of Assyria in 644 B.C. In the treaty, the female deity Pinikir was placed at the head of 37 deities who were invoked. The three chief goddesses, who were the original rulers of the Elamite pantheon, reflected the federal structure of Elam. Pinikir represented

Susiana, while Kirisha, Liyan, and Parti represented Anshan. They gave way in the 2nd millennium to male divinities, but the goddesses were never removed from their place at the head of the pantheon. Numerous Elamite cities had goddesses as divinities. Manzat wife of Siut, one of the earliest gods, protected pregnant women, while the terrifying Lamashtu was responsible for puerperal fever and infant mortality. As discussed earlier, doves made of precious materials, which may have represented the celestial powers of the goddesses, were made as offerings to the deities.

A final note on Elamite religious architecture. Temples were adorned with horns, and ziggurats were generally surmounted by several pairs of horns. This horn element may have originated in the Persian Plateau, but one has to wonder if there was any connection to the "Horns of Consecration" of the Minoans.

CHAPTER EIGHT

CONNECTIONS BETWEEN THE CIVILIZATIONS OF ELAM, THE INDUS VALLEY, AND CENTRAL ASIA

Elam was distinct from the contemporary civilizations of Sumer and that of the Indus Valley in that it integrated large expanses of geographically diverse territory, both politically and culturally. As discussed earlier with respect to a Neo-Assyrian map of Sargon's conquest (2300 B.C.), Elam encompassed the entire Persian Plateau. Elamite cultural influence, however, stretched far beyond in the east, reaching Central Asia and the territories of present-day Afghanistan and Pakistan. Ancient settlements on the eastern edge of what we know as Afghanistan emerged about 5000 years ago and were abandoned a thousand years later. These settlements point to the link between Elam and the Indus Valley Civilization.

Of the hundreds of settlements, three of the larger ones, Shar-i-Sokhta, Shadad, and Konar Sandal, indicate advanced civilizations. Shar-i-Sokhta was close to copper, tin, and turquoise deposits, and lay on the route bringing lapis lazuli from the region of Afghanistan. Proto-Elamite seals have been found here, as well as at Konar Sandal.

Bronzes from the Tedzhen oasis and Bactria in the regions of Central Asia show connections with the animal-style weapons of Susa, as do ceramics, sculpture, and seals.

In addition to the Elamite influence, a major stream of cultural influences from the Indus valley may be observed in these regions. Indus weights, seals, and etched carnelian beads have been found at Konar Sandal. In addition, the ceramics show links with Turkmenistan in Central Asia to the north as well as to the Indus civilization. Excavations in the southern branch of the Amu Darya River (the ancient Oxus) have revealed a group of Indus settlements near Shortugai. The Namazza 5 phase culture in southern Turkmenistan was influenced by the Harappan culture as evidenced by imported seals at Alintempe, and by a writing system similar to the Indus script.

CHAPTER NINE

THE CIVILIZATIONS OF ANCIENT INDIA

1. THE INDUS VALLEY CIVILIZATION

The first ancient India civilization recorded and studied was that of the Indus Valley. This was a Bronze Age culture centered mainly along the Indus River basin as well as along the Ghagger Hakra River, now mainly dried up but which at one time ran parallel to the Indus. The Indus Valley civilization encompassed most of the territories of modern Pakistan, southeastern Afghanistan, Baluchistan in Iran, and the westernmost states of India; it lasted two thousand years from about 3300 to 1300 B.C. It was predated by the Aceramic and Ceramic phases of the Neolithic Age. Archaeological evidence from the Proto-Urban sites of Amri, Kot-diji, Kalibangan, and Mehrgahr point to continuous occupation of the area, without signs of intrusion by new peoples, and suggests that it was an indigenous culture. Mehrgahr, for example, which was strategically placed in terms of trade at the entrance to the Bolan Pass, shows continuous occupation from 7000 B.C. onwards, with evolution in the skills and arts of people up to the Mature Harappan Phase. Evidence also exists of experimentation and innovation rather than the imitation of foreign models.

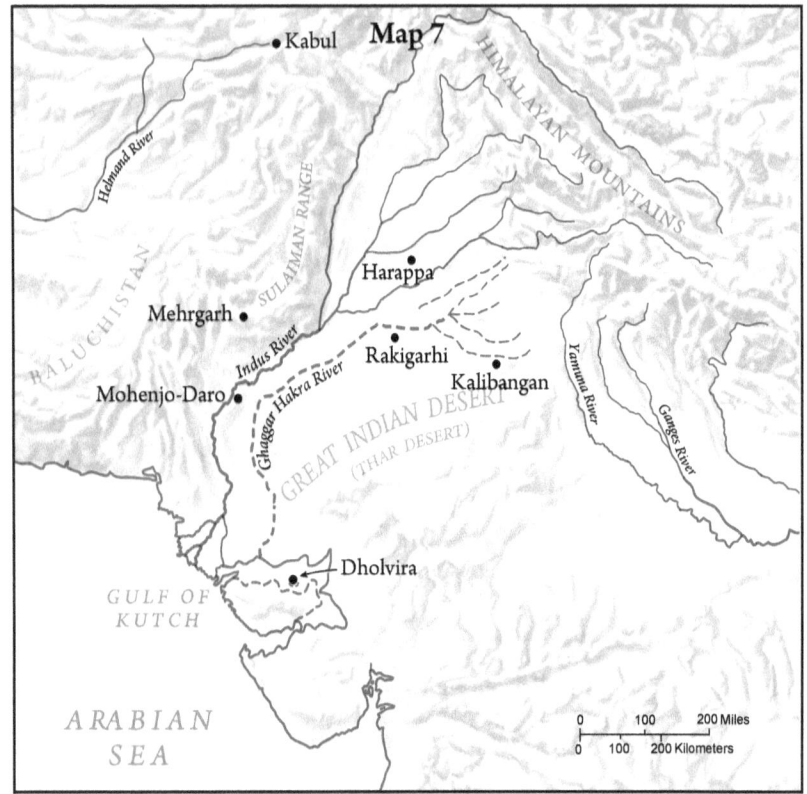

Indus Valley Civilization

The Indus Valley culture is divided into the three following phases, which are called Harappan owing to the name of one of the first cities to be excavated.

1. Early Harappan (3300–2600 B.C.)
2. Mature Harappan (2600–1900 B.C.)
3. Late Harappan (1900–1300 B.C.)

1. EARLY HARAPPAN PHASE (3300–2600 B.C.)

The Early Harappan Phase is also called the Regionalization Period, because agricultural settlements based on wheat, barley, and domestic cattle began to appear. It was also at this time that the Indus script made an appearance.

2. MATURE HARAPPAN PHASE (2600–1900 B.C.)

This was the high point of the civilization, when a sophisticated and technologically advanced culture emerged. Altogether there were about 1500 sites, the largest of which were Harappa, Mohenjo-daro, Dholavira, Rakighari, and Ghanveriwala. They were characterized by a citadel that may have represented centralized authority, and an urban quality of life. Urban planning included a sanitation system—the world's first—with sewerage, drainage, and hydraulic engineering. There were granaries, warehouses, dockyards and protective walls. The Indus people achieved great accuracy in measuring length, mass, and time. Instruments to measure whole sections of the horizon as well as tidal locks were developed. Their engineering skills were remarkable, especially in building docks after a careful study of tides, waves, and currents. They evolved new technologies in metallurgy and worked with copper, bronze, lead, and tin. Trade networks were both internal with related regional cultures and external with distal sources of raw materials. Indus Valley urban centers exported timber, gold, tin, carnelian, and lapis lazuli to various Mesopotamian sites, which may have referred to the Indus Valley as the country of Meluhha. Large numbers of Indus Valley seals have been found at various sites as well as in Mesopotamia, and are intricately and skillfully carved, some showing evidence of writing.

The purpose of the citadels is unknown, because there is no evidence of temples or palaces on them. Nor was the great bath at Mohenjo-daro on a citadel. Some speculate that it might have been used for ritual purification, as in later Hinduism, and had a religious function. It could also have had a recreational and social function like that of the Roman baths. One of the discovered artifacts having a recreational function was the chess board.

It is important to point out that the civilization is remarkable for its relative egalitarianism, low wealth concentration, and access to water and drainage facilities for all houses.

Hypothesized Religion of the Indus Valley Civilization

The religion of the Indus culture is a matter of conjecture, because the Indus script has not been deciphered. Sir John Marshall, one of the early excavators of the Indus culture, made certain inferences from the widespread use of certain kinds of seals, terra-cotta figurines, and pottery. He concluded that the great numbers of female terra-cotta figures were popular representatives of the Great Mother Goddess who became Parvati, the consort of Siva in modern Indian religion and literature. In the same way Marshall concluded that a male figure seated in the yogic position flanked by wild goats and wearing a great horned buffalo headdress with Pipal leaves growing in the center were the attributes of whom we now call Siva. Other recurrent themes were of a tree spirit with animals standing in front of it, and of a row of seven figures standing in front of a Pipal tree. The latter has been identified with the "Seven Rishis" or the "Seven Mothers" of later times.

In addition, certain abstract motifs and symbols anticipate those of later Indian religion. These include the Pipal and banyan trees as symbols of fertility, protection, and death. Bangles are the symbols of family and the long life of the husband. The swastika represents the order of the universe with right and left turning arms, as well as different schools of philosophy. In the later religions of Hinduism and Buddhism, the swastika represented the opposing forces of nature.

3. LATE HARAPPAN PHASE (1900–1300 B.C.)

This was a period of decline. The current thinking is that a natural disaster of great magnitude, not an invasion or invasions, was the cause. The tectonic environment is the collision of the Indian and Eurasian plates, together with the subduction of the Arabian plate beneath the Eurasian plate. In 2001 A.D., a massive earthquake devastated the Kutch region. Based on the evidence of that earthquake, some geophysicists have theorized that the Indus Valley Civilization was overwhelmed by an earthquake and subsequent tsunami. By this theory, the inundation of the Indus and the Ghagger Hakra rivers by a wave traveling up them shifted the course of the latter to the point where it completely dried up. The geological record does show that the Ghagger Hakra, one of the main arteries of trade for the Harappans, dried up in the early 20th century B.C. In addition, the silting of the riverbed regions caused river commerce to become inaccessible. Consequently, the inhabitants began moving to adjoining areas, as well as eastward. The regional cultures that emerged were the Ochre Coloured Pottery Culture (Ganges), the Jukar Culture (Sind), the Cemetery H Culture (Punjab), the Malwas Culture (Madhya Pradesh) and the Banas culture (Rajasthan). They are identified as the non-urban regional cultures of Harappa on account of their pottery, burial patterns, and crafts. Some of these cultures have survived for centuries, keeping intact the non-urban traditions of the Harappan civilization.

2. THE CIVILIZATION OF INDIA FOLLOWING THE ENTRY OF AN INDO-EUROPEAN PEOPLE

The Aryan Migration and Entry into India, Interaction with the Dravidians, and the Resulting Culture

Scholars generally agree that the ancestral home of the Indo-Europeans was in the Eurasian steppes, north and east of the Black Sea and extending to the Caspian Sea. Sometime around 2000 B.C. groups started migrating into areas of present-day Afghanistan and Iran. Their language belonged to the Indo-Iranian branch of Indo- European languages. This branch comprised Indo-Aryan, Iranian, and the related languages of Romani of the Gypsies and Nuristani of the Hindu Kush region of Afghanistan and Pakistan. The staging area, although controversial, appears to have been south of the Aral Sea.

Some of the groups speaking an archaic form of Sanskrit migrated east and west. One of the groups migrating west may became the Kassite rulers of Babylon (1595–1158 B.C.). Their names reveal the names of the two Vedic gods Surya and Marutta, and the Indian name of a king Abirattas. Similarly, the Hurrian Kingdom of Mittani (1500–1300 B.C.) had rulers with Aryan names, and in a treaty with the Hittites they list their gods as the Rigvedic gods Indra, Nasatya, Varuna, and Mitra. There are other examples of the use of Sanskritic words. A treatise on horse training by Kikuli of Mittani used the names of Indic numerals for the courses that a chariot makes around a race track: Aika, Tera, Panza, Satta and Na (one, three, five, seven and nine).

One of the groups migrating east through the Khyber Pass into the Peshawar area reached the Swat Valley region of present-day Afghanistan around 1700 B.C.

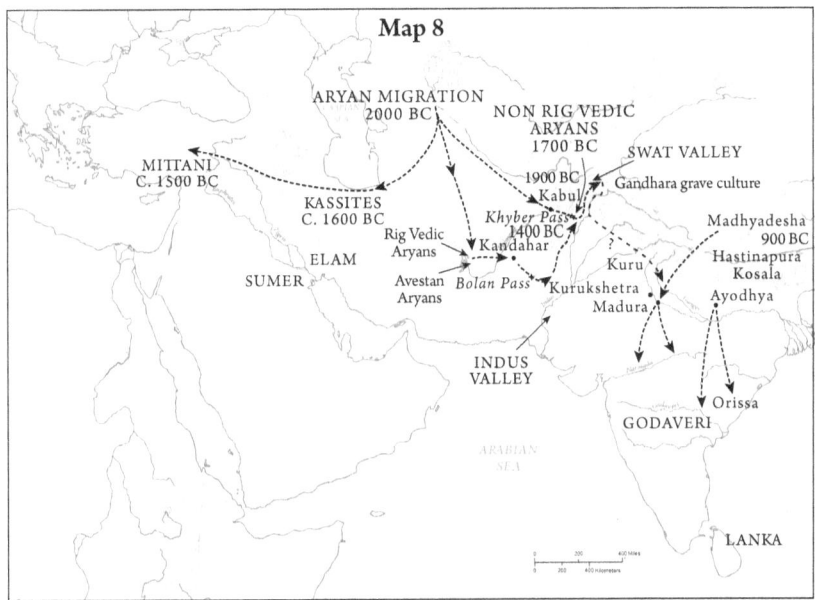

Migrations of the Indo-Aryans

Another group of people migrated into the area of modern eastern Iran and Afghanistan near the lake of the Helmand River about 1700-1400 B.C. Elements within them had common ties of culture, mythology, and ritual, and called themselves "Arya" or "noble." They separated into two groups defined by their sacred texts, the *Avestan* and the *Rigveda*. The language of the Yashts, known from the earliest hymns of the *Avestan*, is very closely related to Sanskrit. The two groups worshipped nature deities and shared both the practice of the use of fire in their rituals and the practice of drinking the juice of a plant (thought to be Ephedra) called *soma* in the *Rigveda* and *haoma* in the *Avestan*. Around 1400 B.C, that is, about 300 years after their non-Rigvedic compatriots, the Rigvedic Aryans entered the Swat Valley after having first passing through the Bolan Pass from the Kandahar region of modern

Afghanistan. They carried with them the collection of sacred hymns and chants they had composed during their long sojourn in the regions of Iran and Afghanistan.

Entry into the Indo-Gangetic basin was through the Swat Valley, which harbored the "Ghandara Grave Culture." Archaeology of this area indicates that the Aryans were intrusive into this region from about 1700 B.C. on, when the first group of non-Rigvedic Aryans arrived. This is evidenced by cultural changes in burial practices and in the type of ceramics used. Burial practices included both inhumation and cremation. As noted earlier on the section on Crete, they practiced a fractional burial rite, by which partial skeletal remains following exposure were deposited in an urn. Burial was with goods of copper, gold, silver, and later on, iron. Horses too were buried with their trappings. This had not occurred in the area before. Grey Ware ceramics similar to those of south Central Asia are another indication of intrusion. The Aryans spoke an early form of Sanskrit that was modified by the language of the original inhabitants to become Classical Sanskrit. It might be said in passing that the Romani language of the Gypsies is also a modified form of Sanskrit. The Gypsies were originally from the Kshatriya (Warrior) caste of northern India. They had been conquered by invading Muslims in the Middle Ages and had followed their conquerors into Europe. The Sanskrit they spoke was modified by each of the countries through which they passed. Likely they were of Aryan origin.

While moving further west into the region of modern-day Iran, the people of the *Avestan* continued to follow the Indo-Iranian religion they had shared with their Rigvedic compatriots. The name "Iran" itself comes from "Arya." Between 1000 B.C. and 600 B.C., the revolutionary religious leader Zarathustra introduced a monotheistic and ethical religion slated to influence other religions. His eschatology about the forces of good and evil and the final struggle became a dominant theme in Christianity. Fire used in the rituals of the Aryans became a supreme symbol in the religion of Zoroastrianism.

THE ARYAN EXPANSION AS CHRONICLED IN THE ANCIENT TEXTS

Ancient texts indicate the timeline of the Aryan expansion into India. The texts also reveal aspects of the culture of their time, together with the impact of the indigenous cultures on the Aryan language, ritual, politics, and society.

1. SETTLEMENT IN THE PUNJAB

The period 1700–900 B.C. is chronicled in the four *Vedas*, together with one of the Vedic commentaries, the *Brahmanas*. The *Vedas* are composed of the *Rigveda* (hymns to be recited), the *Yagurveda* (formulas to be recited by the officiating priest), the *Samaveda* (formulas to be sung), and the *Atharveda* (a collection of spells and incantations).

The Sarasvati River mentioned in the early *Rigveda* is most probably the Helmand River in Afghanistan, and not the Ghagger Hakra River to which the name had been transferred and which had dried up in the early 20th century B.C. The *Avestan* refers to the Helmand River as Haraxvati, which is the cognate of Sarasvati, just as *haoma* is a cognate of *soma*, the juice of the intoxicating plant they used. The text also refers to the river in terms similar to that used in the *Rigveda*. Moreover, the Helmand River flows into a terminal lake as described in both the *Avestan* and the *Rigveda*, while the Ghagger Hakra River, before drying up, flowed into the ocean.

From the *Rigveda* we learn that the Aryans first settled in the Punjab, vanquished an indigenous people whom they referred to as Dasyus, and changed from a pastoral life style to an agricultural one. They refer to the Dasyus with pejorative terms such as "noseless," "bull lipped," "black devils," and "cattle thieves." The Dasyus were not the inhabitants of the Indus Valley Civilization but were possibly one of the indigenous tribes of the area. These tribes appear to have been quite advanced in that the Aryans referred to their "Iron Forts." The Aryans themselves were using primitive wooden structures of bamboo at that time.

After much infighting, one of the clans, the Bharata, a branch of the Puru, became dominant by defeating the rest of the clans at the famous Battle of the Ten Kings, which probably took place around the 10th century B.C. Afterwards the center of gravity shifted to Madhyadesha—"The Middle Country."

Vedic Hinduism

The writings of the four *Vedas* together with their commentary the *Brahmanas* compose Vedic Hinduism and are considered to be knowledge born out of Shruti, inspired revelation, as opposed to Smriti, manmade transmitted knowledge. The earliest *Vedas* were considered to have been compiled around 1500 B.C and to have been finally written down in 500 B.C. after centuries of oral transmission. The deities of the *Vedas* are essentially nature gods. The supreme deity of the Indo-Europeans was Zeus, Dyeus in Indic. He was replaced by Indra who had the dual role of warrior god and weather god. Agni was the god of fire, and

Varuna was both the guardian of Rta (cosmic order) and the supreme judge. Appeasement of these powerful gods was through the sacrifice. A Brahman priest would be called in to perform the ceremonies in front of a fire lit at a sacrificial altar. The Brahman priests, who alone knew the rituals and formulae whereby the gods could be brought to the sacrifice, were masters of a great mystery. "Brahman" was the magical power in the sacred utterance, called the "Mantra."

By the end of the Rigvedic period (c. 1100 B.C.), a creator god "Prajapati" or "Brahma" had developed. He was thought of as a primeval man sacrificed by the gods, who were his children. From the body of the divine victim the universe was produced. Thus the priests by means of re-creation of the primeval sacrifice of the creator god would cause the world to be born anew. Without regular sacrifice, all cosmic processes would cease and chaos would reign. So the order of nature ultimately was not dependent on the gods but rather on the Brahman priests. This is the basic doctrine of the *Brahmanas*. The Vedic manuals are in effect instructional manuals for the sacrifice.

In the later Vedic period, the sacrifice was transferred from being an offering to the gods to a celebration of the power of the king. The idea of kingship gradually evolved from that of a clan chieftain "Raja," whose power was controlled by assemblies, to that of a hereditary monarchy. The legitimization of the king's power was confirmed by the lengthy and elaborate rituals of sacrifice conducted by the priests. Vast numbers of animals were slaughtered. The collaboration between the kings and the Brahman priests was instrumental in creating and maintaining the caste system. During this period, the priests (Brahmans) and the kings (Kshatriyas) consolidated their positions. The producers, free peasants, and traders became the third group (Vaishyas). Artisans, laborers and slaves were degraded into the fourth position (Shudras). The first two castes were not necessarily dominated by the Aryans, because many of the learned of the indigenous population were co-opted into them as discussed later. Many of the pre-Aryans who were skilled craftsman and workers fell into the fourth group because of their special skills. However, the word for caste in India, Varna, means color. The greatest stigma was attached to the pollution of the upper castes by the lower. Many modern Hindus find rationalization for the caste system in the *Vedas* very much as the kings of Europe who legitimized and sanctified their power through what they called "the Divine Right of Kings."

2. SETTLEMENT IN THE MADHYADESHA, THE MIDDLE COUNTRY.

The Madhyadesha extended between the Indus and the Ganges Rivers. Events that occurred in this area are chronicled in the epic *Mahabharata*, which is ten times longer than the *Iliad* and the *Odyssey* combined and four times longer than the other epic *Ramayana*. The title *Mahabharata* is translated as the *Great Tale of the Bharata Dynasty*, which was referred to earlier. The Kurukshetra war written about in the epic was a dynastic struggle between cousins, the Kauravas and the Pandavas, for the throne of Hastinapura. It resulted in a battle in which a number of ancient kingdoms participated as rival clans around the 10th century B.C. The affairs of royalty and warfare are the backdrop to the plots of both epics. According to the epics, the honor of the hero, as well as the call to duty as interpreted by Vedic Brahmanism, is the reason for all wars and suffering. The ethics of the *Bhagavad Gita*, a section of the *Mahabharata*, exemplifies the defense of the established order against the reformers. Here the hero Arjuna awaits the beginning of the battle and expresses doubts about fighting when he sees old friends, relatives, and teachers in the enemy ranks. He turns to Krishna his charioteer and asks for advice. The right course of action, he is told, is to be taken according to circumstance without personal consideration. For the Brahman, the virtue is wisdom; for the warrior, valor; for the Vaisya, industry; and for the Sudra, service. By fulfilling his class function to the best of his ability, with devotion to God, a man will find salvation whatever his class.

The post Rigvedic texts and the epics record not only the struggles that went on between Aryan and non-Aryan but also the internecine warfare that occurred between the different Aryan tribes.

3. EXPANSION EAST ALONG THE GANGETIC BASIN.

Expansion along the Ganges valley took place around 900-300 B.C. and is chronicled in the commentaries of the *Vedas*, the *Brahmanas*, the *Aranyakas*, and the *Upanishads*. During this period, as the Aryans migrated east along the Ganges and south to the Deccan Plateau, there was a great deal of interaction between the Aryans and the non-Aryans, especially the Harappans, whom I shall refer to as Dravidians. The rationale for equating the two is given at length in the Language section. As the Aryan advance took place, all ideas of exclusivity were compromised. Not only did the Aryans absorb much of the religious ideas of the sages and intelligentsia of the indigenous culture, but they also engaged in some intermarriage as recorded by the ancient texts, especially by the epics. The Aryans were an illiterate people, and it was to the revered sage Vyasa that attribution of the *Mahabharata* was given. Vyasa was also credited with arranging the *Vedas* into four texts. He was also called Krishna Dvaipajana referring to his dark complexion, as well as to his birthplace, an island.

The *Aranyakas* or *Forest Books* are the concluding portions of the *Brahmanas*. They are transitional between the *Brahmanas* and the *Upanishads* in that they discuss not only rites and magical thinking but also philosophical questions and speculations. The *Forest Books* were referred to as such because ascetics and mystics retreated into the forest together with students to get away from the distraction of urban life and discuss weighty questions. Embedded or supplemental to the *Aranyakas* are the *Upanishads*, which discuss questions of cosmological and personal significance. These are discursive in style, with the student learning at the feet of his master.

In their passage along the Gangetic basin, the Aryans absorbed the doctrines of Samsara (Transmigration) and Karma. Transmigration is the passage of the soul through repeated births while Karma is the philosophy that the form of life taken in rebirth is dependent on one's conduct in the previous life. To some thinkers, the thought of endless birth was a depressing and daunting prospect. The escape from the endless cycle of birth and death was through mystical knowledge achieved by meditation and asceticism.

PHILOSOPHY AND RELIGION
(a) Mysticism and Asceticism
In a later hymn of the *Rigveda*, there is a reference to "The Munis," the silent ones, different from the Brahmans, who appeared to have acquired

transcendental power. Asceticism varied. A range existed from some ascetics who eschewed all material desires and lived a solitary life away from urban settings to some who inflicted extreme measures of self-torture on themselves. Most of the developments in metaphysical thought came about through those ascetics who practiced mental and physical exercises of meditation in order to acquire magical power and freedom from materialistic desires. For the mystics, as their mystical experience deepened, there came transcendental knowledge, freedom, and ultimate salvation. By the time the *Upanishads* were written, asceticism was widespread and the Brahmans could no longer ignore it. The more orthodox teachings of the mystics were collected and added to the *Brahmanas* as *Aranyakas* and *Upanishads*. Still later a system of mystical training called Yoga was added. While the Brahmans incorporated some of the more orthodox aspects of mystical thought into the commentaries, they continued to practice the Vedic sacrifice while maintaining its qualified validity.

One of the main religious constructs of the *Upanishads* was how the individual self or "Atman" could reach union with the "Brahman" or universal soul through meditation or Yoga.

(b) Naturalistic, Agnostic, Atheistic, and Materialistic Cosmogonic Theories

The first millennium B.C. was an age of great intellectual ferment, when questions of cosmology, philosophy, and man's place in the universe were discussed. Some believed that the world began as water, fire, wind, or ether, and that this was the ultimate reality. Others believed, as did the Greek philosopher Democritus, that the earth was made of atoms. Still others believed that that the universe was based on an impersonal principle that included fate (Niyati), time (Kala), nature (Svabhava), or chance (Samgati).

The Dravidian Ajivikas were atheistic and strict determinists who believed the whole universe was determined by fate (Niyati) and that it is impossible to influence the course of transmigration in any way. They developed the Parmedian view (from the Greek philosopher of the 6th century B.C.) that all change is illusory, and that the world is eternally at rest.

Some were Pyrrhonists, who denied the certainty of any knowledge, while materialists denied the existence of the soul. Ajita, a contemporary of the Buddha, founded one of the materialistic schools that flourished during the middle of the 1st millennium B.C. Hindu, Jain, and Buddhist literature devoted much time attacking the Caravakas and the Lokalatas, adherents of two of the materialistic schools. According to their adversaries, the materialistic schools advocated making the most of one's life, and getting what happiness one could get, because religion and morality were futile pursuits. Some secular literature of the day such as the *Arthasastra* and the *Kamasutra* have irreligious undercurrents.

The *Tattvopaplavasimha* (*The Lion Destroying All Religious Truth*) was written by a certain Jayarasi in the 8th century A.D. He was an agnostic who set out to destroy the basic propositions of the chief religions of his day.

(c) Buddhism and Jainism

The two great religions of Buddhism and Jainism arose against the background of the ascetics and the mystics, not in the kingdoms of the time, but in the republican clans. In the kingdoms, there was a close alliance between the Brahmans and the kings, with emphasis on ritual and reaffirmation of the caste system. The Gana Sanghas or Clans were an alternative type of political entity to the kingdoms. Gana means equal and Sangha means assembly. They were spread around the periphery of the Indo-Gangetic Plain on the foothills of the Himalayas in northwestern India, including the Punjab. They rejected the Vedic tradition, suggesting they were of an even older tradition predating the *Vedas* and were of an indigenous origin. Power in the republics rested either in the hands of an oligarchy, or in the heads of clans whose offices were not hereditary, and who presided over an assembly. There was discussion over various issues, and if certain issues could not be resolved they were put to a majority vote. The Gana Sanghas were more tolerant of unorthodox values and individual opinions. In the *Anabasis of Alexander*, the Greek historian Arrian gives an account of how Alexander met free and independent Indian communities at every turn. Two others, the Greek and Roman historians Diodorus Siculus and Rufus Quintus Curtius, writing about Alexander, mention people called the Sarbacae Sambasta, whose form of government was democratic rather than regal. Megasthenes, the Greek ambassador to the Indian emperor Chandragupta Maurya, described the entire northern half of northwestern India as dominated by republics. It was out of these republics that Buddhism and Jainism arose.

The dates of Buddha's life are conventionally accepted to be 563–483 B.C. Born into a noble Kshatriya family he renounced his former life and retreated into the jungles. After a period of meditation, he reached enlightenment and preached all over northern India. He espoused nonviolence, egalitarianism, and the reform of Vedic Brahmanism.

The basic principles of Buddha's philosophy are that sorrow, suffering, and dissatisfaction, referred to by the word *Dhukka*, are inherent in life and can only be eliminated by giving up the cravings of personal ambition, desire, longing, and selfishness of all kinds. The cravings can only be stopped by taking a middle course between self-indulgence and extreme asceticism, and by leading a moral and well-ordered life. In transmigration a new life arises as part of the chain of events which include the old. The state of Nirvana or extinction is achieved through the ideas and methods expounded by Buddha in the Four Noble Truths and the Eightfold Path. The former are The Noble Truth of sorrow, which arises from the concept of individuality; The Noble Truth of the arising of sorrow, which is born of the cravings for sensual pleasure, for continued life, and for power; and The Noble Truth for the stopping of sorrow by extinguishing it through The Noble Truth of the Way, or the Eightfold Path. The latter comprises Right Views, Right Resolve, Right Speech, Right Conduct, Right Livelihood, Right Effort, Right Recollection, and Right Meditation.

Buddhism spread to Southeast Asia through Sri Lanka. This branch known as Hinayana Buddhism is believed by many Buddhists to reflect the essential teachings of the Buddha. The other branch is known as Mahayana Buddhism, which spread through Tibet to China and Japan. Buddhism died out in India around the 11th century A.D., after over a thousand years, for a complex variety of reasons.

The dates of Mahavira, the founder of Jainism, are generally accepted to be 599–527 B.C. Mahavira, too, came from a noble Kshatriya family, renounced his former life, and through meditation worked out his philosophy.

The guiding principles of Jainism reflect a very specific rejection of the temple sacrifices and caste system. At the heart of the Jain doctrine is the principle of Ahimsa (Nonviolence), and the avoidance of killing any form of life, because Jains believe all living things share with mankind the possession of a soul (the Jiva). For Jains, each human life is judged in terms of its accumulated Karma. This is an impurity that weighs down the soul, but a true ascetic can reduce it to nothing, that is, until the soul is unimpeded. He can then achieve Moksha through release from the cycle of rebirth. The annihilation of Karma comes through penance and disciplined conduct. Otherwise the cycle of transmigration continues indefinitely.

Jaina philosophers also developed a view of space and time foreshadowing that of the theory of relativity in modern physics. Unlike Buddhism, Jainism survives in India to this day. The Jains were a highly literate trading community, with a developed sense of business enterprise. They also have maintained a strong theological discipline among themselves.

Gandhi was heavily influenced by the nonviolence, egalitarianism, and rejection of the caste system as purported by Buddhism and Jainism.

(d) Hinduism

The *Puranas* are Hindu story texts composed over several centuries in the 1st millennium A.D. and that were instrumental through the learned persons of two sects, Vaishnavism and Shaivism, in transforming orthodox Brahmanism into popular Hinduism.

For more than a thousand years until the 6th century B.C., Vedic Brahmanism had been the principal religion of north India. During the

Post-Mauryan period (2nd century B.C.) two strongly theistic traditions called Vaishnava and Shaiva evolved. They centered around the concepts of a supreme deity in the form of Vishnu or Siva, with salvation made possible through intense love and devotion to the deity, the process being known as Bhakti. This was, however, practiced within the parameters of a modified form of Vedic Brahmanism in which animal sacrifice was rejected. Vaishnava focused at first on the older deities, Vasudeva, a tribal deity, Narayana, a deity referred to in the *Brahmanas*, and Krishna, a deity of the Yadeva clan. All became identified with Vishnu, a Vedic god of lesser importance. The Shaiva tradition rests upon the ancient deity Shiva and the mother goddess Shakti, Shiva's consort. He is traced by some to the Harappan culture. Others trace him to Rudra in the *Vedas*, a god who represented the destructive and malignant forces of nature. He was elevated to a supreme force in one of the Upanishads.

The third strand of Hinduism was that of the local cults. The most powerful cult, Devi or Shakti, was the worship of the Mother Goddess and her power for doing good or evil. The goddess as Uma or Parvati showed her beneficial nature, while as Durga Kali she assumed her demonic form.

The Tantric cults accorded much strength and respect to the female gender.

One very important aspect of religion that illustrates a way by which the pre-Aryans influenced the Aryans is the ceremony of the Puja. The pre-Aryans invoked a supreme spirit into an object and meditated on it. Then, into their ritual of Puja, the Aryans incorporated their ritual of *soma* associated with fire worship and spirit invocation as an act of thanks to the gods for favors bestowed upon them. It can be noted that in ancient Crete as well, the epiphany of the goddess was invoked through ritual dancing and music and was a major aspect of Cretan religion.

4. EXPANSION SOUTH FROM 900 B.C.

The *Ramayana* chronicles the southward expansion of the Aryans mostly from the eastern Gangetic Basin, as opposed to the *Mahabharata* which chronicles events happening in the western Gangetic Basin. Southward expansion occurred into Madhya Pradesh, Gujarat, Maharashtra, and Orissa. A clan called the Yadus migrated south from Madura in the western basin, while others from Ayodhya in Kosala in the eastern Gangetic Basin migrated south to establish a kingdom on the river Godaveri. As a result, the Dravidians were driven southward. The *Ramayana* is the story of Rama, a claimant to the throne of Ayodhya, who loses his throne through the jealousy of his stepmother, and who was exiled into the jungles. While there, his wife Sita was abducted by Ravanna, the king of Lanka. Attribution was to the author Valmiki, who was reputedly a contemporary of Rama, and who composed the epic around 600 B.C.

INTERACTION OF BRAHMANISM WITH THE DRAVIDIANS

The Dravidians, although having a loose class system, had no caste system. Toward the later centuries of the 1st millennium B.C., Brahmans began to infiltrate south. During this time almost the whole of India, including south India, practiced Buddhism, and there was great resistance to Vedic Brahmanism, especially among the Vellalars, who were wealthy landowners and agriculturists. As the Indian historian and linguist Srinivasa Iyengar has said about Pre-Aryan Tamil culture, "The scheme of four Varnas [ranks of persons in Hindu society] necessary to a people, every detail of whose life is rite, could not well spread among Tamils, whose life for many millenniums previously was secular and based on social democracy." All through the 1st millennium A.D., the kings of south India, whether Pallava, Pandya, Chera, or Chola, encouraged and supported the Brahmans and the temples in order to gain legitimacy for themselves, similar to what happened in the north. They conferred increasingly large land grants upon the Brahmans and the temples. It was not until the 8th century A.D. that the caste system gained a foothold, and the Brahmans allowed the Vellalars to function as temple managers and functionaries. In some respects the system became as oppressive as the one in the north. The lowest strata, the untouchables, were termed Paraya. The term migrated into English as "pariah," meaning outcast.

Unfortunately present-day Tamils identified with their northern compatriots and instituted a rigid caste system that has parallels to slavery, especially for the lowest castes, with upward mobility for the most part being denied.

The Tamils of south India had at one time matriarchal and matrilineal systems, which lasted to relatively recent times. However, in modern times Tamil women in general tend to be denigrated. Upper-class men, too, are enslaved by the rites, rituals, and taboos of their class.

THE UNDERLYING LANGUAGES AND SCRIPTS

THE UNDERLYING LANGUAGE OF LINEAR A

BECAUSE DECIPHERMENT OF the underlying language of the Linear A script is so dependent on the already deciphered Linear B script, an overview of the scripts and languages associated in the decoding of both of them, as well as the factors that went into deciphering Linear B, will be discussed first. Associated scripts and languages will also be briefly discussed. Linear B was adapted from Linear A by the Mycenaean Greeks, and they will be the scripts, together with their underlying languages, to be addressed last.

The following scripts and languages are discussed in the following order.

1. The languages and scripts of ancient Lycia and Caria
2. The Languages and scripts of ancient Elam
3. The Proto-Elamo-Dravidian, the Proto-Dravidian, and the Dravidian languages
4. The language and script of the Indus Valley Civilization
5. The language and scripts of ancient Cyprus
6. The decipherment of the Linear B script and its underlying language
7. The underlying language of the Linear A script

CHAPTER TEN

THE LANGUAGES AND SCRIPTS OF ANCIENT LYCIA AND CARIA

THE LYCIAN AND CARIAN LANGUAGES

As discussed earlier, according to Greek tradition the Lycians originally came from Crete, and they called themselves Termilae and their country Termmissa. The Greek historian Ephorous (4th century B. C.) records that the persons who became the Lycians first emigrated to Caria, where they founded the city of Miletus, after the Cretan city of the same name. (Another tradition holds that Idris in Caria was the first city founded by the Cretans.) The Hittite texts of the Late Bronze Age refer to Millawanda or Milawata as the region of the Lukka communities, Lukka being the name given to the Lycians by the Hittites. These references suggest not only that the Lycians (Termilae) originally came from Crete, but also that the word Lukka refers to the Lycians and not to the Luwians. Moreover, the Boghazkoy archives of the Hittites refer to the Luwians as Luwili.

The references also suggest that Caria was the first point of settlement of the emigrants, and that they moved southward, probably under the pressure of invading tribes. They finally settled in the region of Lycia, displacing the Solymi tribe. They were later joined by Lycus, who was expelled from Athens by his brother, King Aegeus. Supposedly, Lycus gave his name to Lycia. From the chronological table of the Parian Marble, we learn the ascent of Minos to the Knossos throne occurred in the latter part of the 14th century B.C. and that the emigrations of the Cretans to Anatolia took place around the same time.

At this time, the Luwians, closely related linguistically to the Hittites, were settled in the Anatolian Plateau south of the Halys River. According to Hittite sources, the Luwians, who were Hittite neighbors, had settled in a kingdom called Arzawa in western and southern Anatolia. Around 1180 B.C. the Hittite kingdom fell before the onslaught of advancing people, sometimes referred to as the Sea Peoples. The event was vividly described in Egyptian texts: "Khatti, Kizzuwatne, Carcamish, Arzawa and Alasiya [Cyprus] were crushed." As a result, many of the peoples of the central and southern regions of the Anatolian plateau were squeezed into the southeast corner of that region as well as into northern Syria, making small independent states. It was after this displacement that the Luwians migrated into Lycia, either by invitation or by invasion. Around the 3rd century B.C., following Alexander's conquest, the indigenous language of the Lycians was replaced by Greek.

It is widely held by linguists, including specialist Professor Craig Melchart, that Lycian and Luwian form a subgroup within the Anatolian family of the Indo-European languages. The Lycian corpus includes more than 150 inscriptions on stone dating to the 5th and 4th centuries B.C, several centuries after the original settlement of the Lycians, or Termilae. The inscriptions on stone are mainly votive or dedicatory texts. The Letoon Trilingual Stele discovered in 1973 records the founding of a cult for the goddess Leto by the citizens of the city of

Xanthos at a temple a few miles south of town. Inscriptions are written in Lycian A, Greek, and Aramaic, and the stele was instrumental in the partial decipherment of the Lycian language. The Xanthos Obelisk, a pillar tomb, describes the military exploits and building activities of a local dynasty, and is written in Lycian A, Lycian B—also known as Milyan (thought by some to be derived from Miletus)—and Greek, on different sides of the Obelisk.

Lycian A shows an affinity with the Luwian language. However, there are continuing difficulties in understanding it because it has many strange and incomprehensible features.

Lycian B is opaque and even less understood, and it is found in only one other place than the Xanthos Obelisk, a tomb in Antiphellos. Knowledge of grammar and the lexicon is quite limited in Lycian, and some of its words are not found in any other Anatolian language. Historically the indigenous culture of the Termilae had centuries of Greek and Luwian influence, and their language appears to form the substratum of the later Lycian language related to Luwian. Just as the Hittites were linguistically and culturally influenced by the indigenous Hatti, so too the language and culture of Luwian Lycia showed features of the indigenous Termilae. The word Termilae appears to be closely related to the word Tamil.

UNDERLYING FEATURES OF THE LYCIAN LANGUAGE THAT SHOW AN AFFINITY TO THE ELAMO-DRAVIDIAN LANGUAGES AND TO LINEAR A

(1) Phonology

Underlying Lycian is an even older language, the language of Linear A. This applies to the Carian language as well, which is regarded as an Indo-European language related to Luwian, Lycian, and Lydian. In the 3rd century B.C. the Greek language replaced the Lycian language, which from about the 6th century B.C. on had been using an early form of the Rhodian Greek alphabet. However, as Lycian had sounds in the language that could not be fully reproduced by the Greek alphabet, additional letters were introduced. These letters appear to have been borrowed from the Cypro-syllabic and Carian scripts. Some of the additional sounds appear to be syllabic in nature. The Luwian language had only three vowels. This was almost tripled in the Lycian alphabet because of the nasalized vowels. Chart 1 shows the Lycian script with the transliteration of the Lycian letters. The Lycian script has 29 letters. In addition to the vowels, a, e, i, and u, it has the following:

- ā and ē, which functioned as nasalized vowels
- m and n, which appear to be nasal consonants or syllabic nasals that functioned as vowels.

As a result most endings of nouns and verbs in Lycian have nasal vowels instead of the vowel+n of Luwian.

The Elamite language will be taken up later, but it is appropriate to discuss the following here because of its relevance.

Matthew Stolper, writing about Elamite, says that spelling variations such as

- Hu-ban ~ Hu-um-ban (a divine name),
- Te-em-ti ~ Te-ep-ti, "lord" and
- Na-ra-an-da, Na-ra-an-te, ~ Na-ra da, Na ra te, "daily"

suggest the existence of nasalized vowels.

CHART 1. The Lycian and Carian Alphabets

LYCIAN ALPHABET				CARIAN ALPHABET				Some Undeciphered Letters
a	⋏	n	∧	a	A	ñ	Φ	日
e	↑	m̃	X	d	C	x	X	⋀
b	B	ñ	∓	l	△	n	Y	X̄
β	⋔	u	O	ü	E	p	⋀⋀	)(
g	Y	p	⌐	r	F	š	⊕	X
d	△	ks	◇	λ	I	l	Ð	
l	E	r	P	q	⊕	e	□	
w	F	s	ς	b	Γ	w/a	ᛘ	
z	I	t	T	m	N	k	▽ Y	
θ	X	γ	Ƴ	o	O	ü	Ⅲ	
γ	l	ā	⋈	t	Q	l	⋈	
k	K	ē	Ƴ̈	š	Þ	γ	↑	
q	✷	h	+	s	M	w/a	ı¦ı	
l	∧	x	V	u	T Y			
m	⋀							

ā and ē are nasalized vowels

m̃ and ñ are syllabic nasals or nasal consonants that function as vowels

The modern Tamil syllabary has five nasalized syllables in the n series. Its relevance will be discussed in the section on the decipherment of Linear A.

- ங	as (ng)	Velar nasal
- ஞ	as (nj)	Palatal nasal
- ண	as (N)	Retroflex nasal
- ந	as (n)	Dental nasal
- ன	as (n)	Alveolar nasal

(2) Verbal morphology

Lycian B has reduplicated verb stems in the present as shown:

- Dditi: (verb) Pres. 1st sg.
- Zazati: (verb) Pres. 3rd sg.
- Kikiti: (verb) Pres. 3rd sg.

In Elamite, too, there are reduplicated verb stems in the present and single ones in the past tense, as the following examples show:

- Li >Lili (give, deliver)
- Tallu > Tatallu (write)
- Kut (carry) Kukt (carry much, frequently)

Lycian has two tenses and two moods: indicative and imperative. The infinitive ends in "ana" as in the following:

- kTTäna (to give birth) and Kbane (to surrender).

In Elamite, stems with n or na are non-past or imperfect infinitives, e.g.:

- Middle Elamite: *Kukkunum pittena* The god commanded me to make an enclosure of (?) the K
- Achaemenid Elamite: *Tuppi talli ma-n-a* I ordered an inscription to be written

(3) Lexicon

Some words in Lycian are not found in any other Anatolian Indo-European tongues.

From the above, parallels between Lycian, Elamite, and the Dravidian language of Tamil can be seen.

(4) Numerical system

This has parallels within the Linear A script. Lycian has vertical lines for numbers 1 to 4 and an O for 10

- |, ||, |||, ||||, O

THE CARIAN LANGUAGE

Achaean Greeks arriving in small numbers on the coast of Anatolia in the Late Bronze Age found it occupied by a non-Greek speaking people. After the fall of the Hittite Empire around 1180 B.C., there was an influx of Ionian and Dorian Greeks who referred to the Carians as speaking a barbarian language. The writings of the ancient Carians did not survive, but several hundred years later, in the 7th century B.C., bilinguals began to appear. There is a question about one of the bilinguals being the same language spoken by the ancient Carians. The script, too, of this period remains obscure, because although Carians were using an alphabetic script similar to that of ancient Greek, many of the morphologically similar letters have different phonetic values. Carian script used a total of 45 letters, with about half of the signs fairly well established. The script, however, remains largely undeciphered. The reason Lycian and Carian appear to be incomprehensible is because Luwian is the overlay to the underlying Elamo-Dravidian language.

Both the Lycian and Carian scripts are shown in Chart 1.

CHAPTER ELEVEN

THE LANGUAGE AND SCRIPTS OF ANCIENT ELAM

As shown in the earlier historical section, "Haltamti," the name by which the Elamites referred to themselves, can be translated as "Land of the Tamils." Also as discussed earlier there is controversy over the meaning of the suffix "ti," which is found on verbs of all periods. Hallock and McAlpin believe "ti" marks finality or completeness; for others (Hinz and Koch) it marks past time, and for still others (Grillot-Susini and Roche; Vallat) anteriority with respect to another verb. However, in this context, which predates the Middle and Achaemenid periods of Elam, it could possibly mean "Land of the Ancient Tamils."

THE ELAMITE SCRIPTS

From the 8th millennium B.C. the development of writing in Elam paralleled that of Sumer. Around the 3rd millennium B.C. a new script appeared in Elam, unlike the cuneiform script that was prevalent in Mesopotamia. Intrusion into the area from the Persian Plateau is suggested by similarities in ceramic technology and architectural styles. Three different scripts developed during the historical period of Elam.

(1) The Proto-Elamite Script (3050 - 2900 B.C.)

About 1500 texts written on clay tablets have been found over a very wide area extending from Elam to the borders of present-day Afghanistan and Pakistan. All Proto-Elamite texts appear to be accounting records, because numbers are preceded by one or more non-numerical signs that are logograms or possibly syllobograms. Controversy surrounds whether the Proto-Elamite tablets represented the Elamite language, and this will be discussed later. The prefix "Proto" is used by scholars because the script preceded a much later script known as Linear Elamite.

The context of many texts is known, because the majority of numerical signs and some ideograms are similar to those of Mesopotamian cuneiform.

The texts appear to show that a sexagesimal and a bisexagesimal numerical system identical to that of the Proto-Cuneiform texts from Mesopotamia were in use. They also appear to have used a decimal system with no parallel in Mesopotamian texts. The sexagesimal system was limited to inanimate objects, while the bisexagesimal system was used to enumerate barley products. The decimal system was used to count humans and animals. Unlike the Proto-Cuneiform texts from Mesopotamia, Proto-Elamite texts were written in a linear script (as was Linear Elamite, but the two should not be confused), had headings without the final total, and had ideograms that were followed by a numerical notation. In Proto-Cuneiform the colophon similar to the headings of Linear Elamite were shown together with the final total on the opposite side of the tablet, and ideograms followed the numerical notations. These elements in the Proto-Elamite script were similar to that of the Linear A script. The script, however, remains largely undeciphered, mainly due to the lack of a bilingual text.

(2) Linear Elamite Script (2250 - 2230 B.C.)

Known from 18 inscriptions on stone and clay objects, and from one on a silver vase, Linear Elamite script appears to be a logo-syllabic script of about 140 signs used by the ruler Puzur Insusinak for a brief period around 2250 B.C. Most of the inscriptions are from Susa, but one was found in Fars and another in southwestern Iran, demonstrating its wide distribution. Such a distribution could mean the language was being spoken over a broad area.

Linear Elamite script has been partially deciphered on account of a bilingual in Old Akkadian. Opponents of those who say that the same language is represented in the two scripts, Proto-Elamite and Linear Elamite, point to the lack of graphic similarities and to the lack of success in attempting to substitute Linear Elamite values for the few graphically similar signs in Proto-Elamite. Moreover, a period of about 800 years stretches between the appearance of the two scripts, and there is little evidence that Linear Elamite evolved from Proto-Elamite. Different scripts can be used to write the same language. For example, the Mycenaean Greeks used the Linear B script for their Mycenaean dialect, while the Greeks of the Homeric age used the modified Phoenician alphabet for their respective dialects. The same applies to Linear Elamite and Cuneiform Elamite, by which different scripts reflected the same language.

(3) Cuneiform Elamite (various dates)

The period between the time when the Proto-Elamite script was no longer in use and the appearance of the Linear Elamite script was not a "silent" period. In Khuzestan, Akkadian cuneiform was in use, having been earlier adapted for the Elamite language around 2500 B.C. Only the syllabic signs were borrowed, however, while the word signs were abandoned. Doing so created a radically simplified writing system, which remained in use until 1500 B.C. This type of cuneiform script is so rare that many aspects of the underlying language remain obscure (the existing samples merely list the names of kings and their capital cities). For the next thousand years the Sumerian or Babylonian languages were used in Elam.

In the latter half of the 2nd millennium B.C. the Elamites readapted the cuneiform script once again to write their language. But Elamite used only 145 of the 700 cuneiform signs used by the Mesopotamians. In the 5th century B.C. the Persian King Darius I of the Achaemenid dynasty used Elamite as the first language for formal inscriptions, and it was originally the only language carved on the famous rock inscriptions of Behistun. Later it was accompanied by Old Persian and Aramaic that constituted the court languages

The Elamite corpus can be divided chronologically and typologically into the following groups:

1. *Old Elamite 2600–1500 B.C.* Written in early Elamite cuneiform exemplified by the treaty of Naram Sin.
2. *Middle Elamite 1500–1000 B.C.* Scattered texts from Khuzestan attest the reigns of two dynasties of the kings of Anshan and Susa.
3. *Neo-Elamite 1000–550 B.C.* Written in readapted cuneiform, it represents a transition in structure between Old Elamite and Achaemenid Elamite.

4. *Achaemenid Elamite 550–330 B.C.* This was a period of Achaemenid domination, with Elamite being the first language used for formal inscriptions.

A very brief overview of the Elamite language is given as follows.

Like Linear B, which was ill adapted to reproduce the sounds of Mycenaean Greek, Akkadian cuneiform was ill adapted to reproduce the sounds of the Elamite language. As a result the phonology is poorly understood.

(a) Phonology

Elamite had at least the vowels /a/, /i/, /u/, and perhaps /e/. The consonants included the stops /p/, /t/, and /k/, the sibilants /s/, /s/ and /z/, the nasals /m/ and /n/, and a fricative /h/.

(b) Morphology

Elamite is an agglutinative and predominantly suffixing language. The inflectional system is based on a relatively small number of nominal and verbal suffixes and clitics.

(c) Nominal morphology

Complex noun phrases are built up from pronoun-like affixes that agree with the head noun along various dimensions of persons and animateness. Personal class distinctions correspond to 1st, 2nd, 3rd person and plural. The agreement suffixes distinguish three classes of inanimate nouns.

Third person nouns are derivative. The animates indicate agent nouns, e. g. *huttira* "maker" or members of a class, e. g. *Babira*, "Babylonian." The inanimate *-me* indicates abstracts, e. g. *takkime* "life."

TABLE 1. Gender, person, and number

		Sing.	Plural	Examples
Animate	1st pers.	-k	-k	sunki-k "I, a king"
	2nd pers.	-t	-t	hutta-n-t "you, doing"
	3rd pers.	-r -θ	-p	nap-ir "he, god"
				nap-ip "they gods"
Inanimate		-me		sunki-me "kingdom, kingship"
		-t		hala-t "mudbrick"
		-n -θ		siya-n "temple"

Suffixes referring to the head are appended to the modifiers, whether they are another noun like a possessor or an adjective, e. g. *u sunki-k Hatamti-k* "I the king of Elam."

(d) Verbal morphology

The verb base can be simple or reduplicated, and can function as a verbal noun or infinitive. Finite verbs have three forms of functioning called conjugations. The finite form or Conjugation 1 has endings special to verbs, and is used in past tense clauses. The participle forms, Conjugations 2 and 3, correspond to non-past clauses and can also be used as nouns and modifiers. They are formed by adding suffixes that mark person gender and number in nouns. All three conjugations distinguish between three persons and two numbers.

The optative marker -ni (may) is the most frequent clitic. The second person of Conjugation 1 serves as the imperative. Prohibitives are Conjugation 3 forms preceded by the particle *anu- ani*.

The word order is subject-object-verb (SOV) with indirect objects preceding direct objects. Some elements of the Elamite grammar have

TABLE 2. Conjugations

Conjugations 1-3 utilize *kulla-* "pray"; *hap(i)-* "hear"; *hutta-* "do"; *tahha-* "help"

Conjugation I (verbal)		Conjugation 2 (base + k) Perfect Participle Nominal conjugation		Conjugation 3 (base + n) Imperfect Participle Nominal conjugation	
Singular	*Plural*	*Singular*	*Plural*	*Singular*	*Plural*
1st pers.					
-h	-hu	-k -k		-n -k	
kulla-h	kullah-hu	hutta-k-k		hutta-n-k	
2nd pers.					
-t	-h-t	-k -t		-n -t	
hap-t	hutta-h-t	hutta-k-t		hutta-n-t	
3rd pers.					
-š	-h-š	-k-r	-k-p	-n-r	-n-p
hutta-š	hutta-h-š	hutta-k-r	hutta-k-p	hutta-n-r	tahha-n-p

already been discussed, together with that of Lycian. Others will be discussed with the grammar of Linear A.

The references for detailed analyses of the Elamite language are listed in the bibliography.

CHAPTER TWELVE

THE PROTO-ELAMO-DRAVIDIAN, PROTO-DRAVIDIAN, AND DRAVIDIAN LANGUAGES

PROTO-ELAMO-DRAVIDIAN

Proto-Elamo-Dravidian is a hypothesized language family that links the Proto-Dravidian languages of India to the extinct Elamite language of ancient Elam. In "Proto-Elamo-Dravidian: The Evidence and its Implications" (*Transactions of the American Philosophical Society*, vol. 71 part 3, 1981), linguist David McAlpin, the chief proponent of this theory, laid out evidence for making the linkage. He demonstrated systematic correlations between Proto-Dravidian and Proto-Elamite in phonology, morphology, and lexicon, and theorized that they were cognate in nature. He also theorized that the lexical evidence pointed to Dravidian and Elamite having separated relatively late in west Asia, presumably in the area of present-day Iran. Later I shall present the evidence that the languages existed over a much wider area.

McAlpin reconstructed Proto-Elamo-Dravidian showing a common stockbreeding vocabulary and traced special developments in agricultural terminology of the Dravidian branch as it pushed into

India. The common word for brick in P.E.D. disintegrated in the 5th millennium B.C. McAlpin theorized that Elamite separated from Proto-Elamo-Dravidian before 3000 B.C. and probably did so after 5500 B.C. He also presented arguments for the reinterpretation of Brahui, which is traditionally assigned to the Northern Dravidian subgroup of the Dravidian languages. According to McAlpin, Brahui would actually appear to be historically and geographically intermediate between the two groups and could be seen as an independent third branch of Proto-Elamo-Dravidian, possibly closer to Elamite. The cognation of Elamite and Dravidian has further implications for the study of the Harappan civilization. The circumstantial evidence for identifying the language of the Indus valley with Elamite or Dravidian has been greatly strengthened by McAlpin's work

PROTO-DRAVIDIAN AND THE DRAVIDIAN LANGUAGES

Starting with Caldwell's *Comparative Grammar of the Dravidian Languages* (1875), linguists have reconstructed a fragment of Proto-Dravidian. There are ten vowels—five short and five long—and sixteen consonants. While any of the five vowels may appear in a root, only a, i, and u may appear in a derivative suffix. Morphology is transparent, agglutinating, and exclusively suffixal. There are two parts of speech, noun and verb. Nouns inflect for case, person, number, and person. There are eight cases, two numbers—singular and plural—and two genders, animate and inanimate. Verbs inflect for tense and mood. There are two tenses, past and non-past, and the two moods are modal and indicative. The basic word order is subject-object-verb (SOV). This is a brief overview; a more detailed one is given by the linguist Sanford B. Steever (see reference in the bibliography).

The Dravidian language family comprises about 25 languages spoken by about 175,000,000 people, mainly in Southeast Asia. They are spoken mainly in southern, but also in central and eastern India. Outside India, Dravidian languages are also spoken in Sri Lanka, Pakistan, Nepal, and the Maldives. Of the four major languages—Tamil, Telagu, Kannada, and Malayalam—all have histories recorded in epigraphy and literature, Tamil being the oldest attested language. The earliest records of Tamil, written in the Asokan Brahmi script, appeared in India by the 5th century B.C. but the fact that it had many local variants even in the early texts suggest that its origins lie even further back in time. It is a syllabic script. None of the theories about the origin of the Brahmi script has proven satisfactory. These include hypothesizing derivation from the West Semitic, the Southern Semitic, or the Indus scripts.

A brief overview of the grammar of Old Tamil as represented by the Tolkappiyam, an early work on Tamil grammar beginning from the 1st century B.C., is given as follows:

(a) Phonology

There are ten vowels—five short and five long—two diphthongs /ai/ and /au/, and seventeen consonants. In addition, there are two allophones—the velar nasal [n] and the fricative [h]—that appear as allophones of other nasals and of /v/ respectively.

(b) Morphology

Old Tamil is predominantly agglutinative and exclusively suffixal.

(i) Nominal morphology. Nominals are primarily inflected for case and number and secondarily for gender and person. There are eight

cases: nominative, accusative, dative, instrumental, equative, genitive, locative, and vocative.

(ii) Verbal morphology. Finite verbs consist of a verb stem, tense marker, and personal ending. There are two tense—past and non-past. In the negative, finite verbs consist of a verb stem, negative marker, and personal ending.

Nonfinite verbs consist of primary forms, secondary forms, and verbal nouns. In primary forms a suffix is added to the verb stem. Secondary forms add a clitic to a primary form.

Verbal nouns are nominalized forms that may be inflected for case.

Two minor parts of speech are adjectives and adverbs.

(e) Syntax

Old Tamil is a head final, SOV language. It is also a pro-drop language.

CHAPTER THIRTEEN

THE INDUS SCRIPT

ALTHOUGH THE MAJORITY of scholars in the fields of linguistics and archaeology theorize that the language and culture of the Indus civilization is Dravidian, dissenting voices claim it is Aryan. The other language family indigenous to India is the Munda family spoken largely in eastern India and related to some Southeast Asian languages. The reconstructed vocabulary of the early Munda does not reflect the Harappan culture.

If one looks at the time frame alone, it would rule out Aryans as a candidate for the Indus civilization. The mature urban phase of the Harappan civilization lasted from 2600 to 1900 B.C. However, the antecedent to this phase, the early Harappan, was in the making at least a thousand years before 2600 B.C, and in Mehrgarh it was in the making from 7000 B.C on.

A number of undifferentiated Indo-Iranian speaking groups, mainly pastoralists with their cattle, had migrated from the Eurasian Steppes around 2000 B.C. One branch speaking an early form of Sanskrit might have reached the Indus as early as 1700 B.C. Linguistic experts believe the Rigveda was first compiled in the Afghanistan area, because the early parts of the texts include references to area places, rivers, and animals. By the time the Aryans had migrated into the area of the Indus Valley Civilization (IVC), that civilization was in decline and the inhabitants had moved into other settlements. John Marshall, one of the early archaeologists of the Indus civilization, has pointed out that the society portrayed in the Vedas is that of a partly pastoral and partly agricultural people who had not emerged from the village state and who had no knowledge of life in cities or of the complex economic organization that such life implies. Their houses were non-descriptive affairs constructed largely of bamboo. The cities of the Indus, however, were densely populated with houses of brick, together with sanitation, bathrooms, and other amenities.

Other factors which militate against the IVC being primarily Aryan are:

1. The female element appears to be coequal with the male or even predominant in the IVC. But in the Vedic pantheon, the female element is almost wholly subordinate to the male.
2. Militaristic equipment such as chariots with the spoked wheel and defensive armor, helmets, and coats of mail, all central element of Aryan culture, are absent in the IVC.
3. The use of gold, copper, and bronze was preferred among the Aryans, as opposed to silver, which was primarily used in the IVC.
4. The cow being prized as opposed to the bull, and the absence of the tiger and the elephant, distinguish the Aryan culture from the Indus culture.
5. The linguistic evidence. McAlpin's view that Brahui, spoken in adjoining areas of Afghanistan and Iran as well as in Baluchistan, is intermediate between Elamite and Dravidian strengthens the

argument that the IVC was Dravidian. Survival of place names is generally a good indicator of the linguistic prehistory of the region. Several place names in the northwestern region of India, like Nagara, Palli, Pattana, and Kotta have Dravidian etymologies.

Moreover, the Rigveda contains not only Dravidian loan words, but also a dramatic increase of them in post-Rigvedic literature. In addition, the Rigveda contains phonological and syntactical Dravidisms. In particular:

1. Retroflex phonemes
2. The gerund
3. The quotative
4. Onomatopoeic constructions.

All of these are absent from the closely related Iranian branch of the Aryan language.

THE INDUS SCRIPT

The main corpus of Indus script writing is in the form of about two thousand seals. The texts are very short; the average number of seals is five and the longest 26. The maximum number of symbols is about 400, of which about 200 are basic signs and the rest ligatures, suggesting that it is a logophonetic script, in which signs are used both for their meanings as well as for their phonetic value.

Another possible indication of an underlying Dravidian language in the Indus texts is from structural analysis that suggests agglutination. Sign groups have the same initial sign but different final signs. The number of these final signs range between 1 and 3. The final signs possibly represent grammatical suffixes that modify the word, and the entire clusters of suffixes would therefore put the word through a series of modifications. Many suffixes in agglutinative languages correspond to a single inflectional ending in an inflected language like that of the Indo-Europeans.

THE NUMERIC SYSTEM

Numbers are represented by vertical lines up to seven. This suggests that the Indus script was base eight, which is very rare, and which has been discussed earlier in relation to Crete.

A frequent pictorial sign in the script resembles a fish. The word for fish (*min*) is also the word for star (homonym). The analogy with the name Min (os) the ruler of Crete is striking.

Asko Parpola, an expert in Indus script, theorizes that pictograms with numerals represented astronomical symbols, which were looked upon as gods in ancient India. The stars were conceived of as fish representing gods swimming in the ocean of heaven.

Chart 2 gives the theorized meanings of the symbols by Parpola and Iravatham Mahadevan, another expert in the field.

CHART 2. The Indus Script

Parpola's interpretation of the Script

Sign	Dravidian Phonetics	Commentary
	Meen = fish or star	The heavenly bodies were conceived of as fish swimming in the ocean of heaven representing stars
	Elu + meen = seven fish or stars	The name of Ursa Major in Tamil
	mey + meen = roof + fish	The name of Saturn in Tamil. Saturn rides a turtle, a fish with a roof
	Vata+meen = fig tree+ fish	In Dravidian the North Star
	Nal+ vata = 4 + fig tree	Representing the Banyan tree, with ropes hanging down

Mahadevans Interpretation of the Script

Sign	Ideographic meaning	Commentary
	jar meaning priest	Frequent terminal sign in the script and connected to the legend of "jar born" sages.
	Lance meaning warrior	Also a terminal sign perhaps a suffix associated with names or titles

CHAPTER FOURTEEN

THE SCRIPTS AND LANGUAGES OF ANCIENT CYPRUS

⌽

A. CYPRO-MINOAN

Cypro-Minoan is writing of the Cypriot Bronze Age. It was named by archeologist Arthur Evans who assumed a link between Linear A and the Cypriot script. Cypro-Minoan was used between 1600 and 1050 B.C. and was presumed to be ancestral to the Cypriot Syllabary. Cypro-Minoan has been classified into four different scripts. The earliest of these, Archaic Cypro-Minoan, shows the greatest similarities to Linear A and was used toward the end of the 16th Century B.C. The other three scripts Cypro-Minoan 2 and 3, were used toward the end of the Bronze Age. Cypro-Minoan 2 has also been found at Ugarit, and Cypro-Minoan 4 was found exclusively at Ugarit. Cypro-Minoan has not been deciphered because of the lack of bilinguals and the small corpus of documents.

B. CYPRIOT SYLLABARY

The decipherment of the Cypriot Syllabary was made by a series of scholars but chiefly by George Smith, an Assyriologist, and by Moriz

Schmidt, a specialist in Greek. By means of a Phoenician-Cypriot bilingual on a votive inscription called the Idalion Tablet (478–470 B.C.), Smith was able to discern that the writing was syllabic, and that it was an inflected language resembling Latin and Greek. Schmidt confirmed that the Cypriot Syllabary was Greek and published his work in 1871; within two years scholars had worked out the entire syllabary.

One theory maintains that Mycenaean Greeks fleeing the Trojan war around the 12th century B.C. settled in Cyprus and adapted the Cypro-Minoan script in order to write their language. However, the Mycenaeans of that time were using the Linear B script both on the mainland of Greece as well as on Crete. The Cypriot Syllabary and the Linear B script are similar in structure and underlying language, which suggests that both were derived from Linear A. The links between Linear B and the Eteo-Cypriot language—one thought to have been spoken by the indigenous population—are discussed below. The writings were originally found only on dedicatory and funerary texts dating to the 11th century B.C. Instances of longer historical texts occurred in Classical times when the Cypro-Syllabic script coexisted with the Greek alphabet. It was abandoned in the 2nd Century B.C. only after Hellenization by Alexander of Macedon in the 4th century B.C.

The Cypro-Syllabic script was used to write two languages, the Greek language and Eteo-Cypriot. One of the languages of the Cypro-Syllabic script was found to be the Arcadio-Cypriot dialect of Greek thought to be derived from Mycenaean Greek and spoken in Arcadia on the Peloponnese and in Pamphylia, which is modern Antalya in Anatolia. The Cypriot Syllabary and the Linear B script were found to have eight morphologically similar signs. Ventris took over their phonetic values and assigned them to the syllabic grid he was designing, an action that became one of the factors used in his deciphering of Linear B. Unlike Linear B, however, the Cypriot script had no logograms.

The Cypriot Syllabary is a syllabic script of 56 signs, but like the Linear B script to be discussed later it could not reproduce all the sounds of the Mycenaean Greek language. So certain spelling conventions were developed, and orthographic simplification was made.

For example,

1. [k] represented initial [k] as well as [g] and [kh]
   [p] represented initial [p] as well as [b] and [ph]
   [t] represented initial [t] as well as [d] and [th]

2. All the signs in the syllabary represent syllables of the open type CV (C = consonant; V = vowel) similar to that in Linear B. However, the Mycenaean Greek language had initial consonant clusters CCV, ending consonants CVC and diphthongs CVV.

(a) In initial consonant clusters all the consonants except the one closest to the vowel were represented by syllable (CV) signs whose vowel agrees with the vowel ending of the final consonant of the cluster. An exception is that nasal consonants such as [m] and [n] preceding another consonant are omitted as shown below.

- E.g.: a-to-ro-po-se spelling for anthropos (human)

(b) Similarly in word ending consonants all the consonants except the one closest to the vowel were represented by syllable (CV) signs whose vowels agrees with the vowel ending of the final consonant.

Again the nasal consonant exception applies. The second exception apllies to word ending consonants where only the sounds of [n], [s], and [r] could appear at the end of a word. They are marked by a silent e as in ne, se, and re, e.g., as shown above in the word a-to-ro-po se

(c) Diphthongs such as ae, au, and ei were spelled out completely.

By contrast Linear B often omitted sounds in initial consonant clusters, ending consonants, and diphthongs.

- E.g.: a-to-ro-qo represented the spelling for anthropos

3. There is no disambiguation between /d/ and /t/ but there is disambiguation between /l/ and /r/. The opposite is true of Linear B.

C. THE ETEO-CYPRIOT LANGUAGE.

Eteo-Cypriot refers to the language attested to by some inscriptions found in Cyprus dating from the 7th to the 4th Century B.C. Although the name Eteo-Cypriot refers to the language of the autochthonous inhabitants of the island of Cyprus, it appears to be a late development. The most famous Eteo-Cypriot inscription, the Amanthus Bilingual, is a bilingual text inscribed in black marble dating to around 600 B.C. and written in the Attic dialect of ancient Greece and in Eteo-Cypriot. The following are the syllabic values assigned to it by the Cypriot Syllabary.

1. A-na   ma-to-ri   U-mi-e-sa-i   mu-ku-la-i   la-sa-na
2. A-ri-si-to-no-se   a-ra-to-wa-na-ka-so-ko-se   ke-ra-ke-ru-to-lo-se
3. Ta-ka-na-ku-no-so-ti   a-lo-ka-i-li-po-ti

The " i " endings in Lines 1 and 3 and the "ose" ending in Line 2 as well as the ti endings in Line 3 may be suffixes.

Transliterated Greek Text: The polis of Amathusians, to Ariston (son of) Aristonax, nobleman.

Some believe the so called Eteo-Cypriot language may be related to the Etruscan and Lemnian languages. This hypothesis is given some credence because of the word la-sa-na. There is r/l confusion in Linear B, even though the Cypriot Syllabary had separate syllables for r and l. Also there is another Mycenaean Greek word appearing in the text. This word is Wanaka, which in Linear B refers to Wanax or King. The Eteo-Cretans appear to have used Linear B Greek with its spelling conventions, including the lack of r/l disambiguation. Taking into consideration the r/l confusion in Mycenaean Greek, the word la-sa-na may be ra-sa-na. Rasenna was the name by which the Etruscans referred to themselves. The text itself bears little resemblance to the language of Linear A.

Overall there is some evidence that the Cypriot Syllabary may be more related to the Linear B script than to Cypro-Minoan.

The Cypriot script together with the eight signs that resembled the signs of Linear B is shown in Chart 3.

CHART 3. The Cypriot Syllabary

The Cypriot Syllabary										
a	✳	e	✳	i	✳	o	⋎	u	↑
ja	◯					jo	᭝		
ka	↑	ke	⤬	ki	⇞	ko	⋂	ku	✳
la	⋎	le	8	li	≤	la	+	lu	⌒
ma	⋇	me	⤫	mi	⋎	mo	⊕	mu	⋈
na	T̄	ne	|ϟ|	ni	⤋	no	⁄⁄	nu	⟩⟩
pa	ǂ	pe	ϟ	pi	⋎	po	ϟ	pu	⋎
ra	Ω	re	⇞	ri	⤴	ro	⋎	ru	)(
sa	V	se	⊢	si	⇞	so	⋎	su	⋈
ta	⊢	te	⤋	ti	↑	to	F	tu	𝔽
wa	⋈	we	I	wi	)(	wo	⤴		
xa	)(	xe	⊣			zo	⋇		
qa	⋇								

Homomorphic Signs		
Linear B	Cypriot	Cypriot sounds
✝	+	lo
Ȳ	T̄	na
ǂ	ǂ	pa
⌐	ϟ	po
⊫	⊢	se
⊢	⊢	ta
⋂	↑	ti
Ŧ	F	to

CIVILIZATIONS OF THE UNCONSCIOUS

CHART 4. The Scripts of Ancient Crete

Creten Seals

The Phaistos Tablet

The Phaistos Disc

The Linear B Script

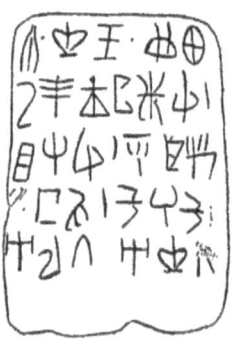

The Linear A Script

CHAPTER FIFTEEN

THE DECIPHERMENT OF THE LINEAR B SCRIPT

LINEAR B INSCRIPTIONS have been found at Knossos, Khania, Armeni and Mallia on Crete, and at Mycenae, Tiryns, Pylos, Thebes and other sites on the Greek mainland. There are about 6,000 inscriptions, 98% of which are engraved on clay tablets, sealings, and nodules. The rest are painted on terracotta vases destined for trading olive oil and wine. The Linear B script was deciphered in 1952 by the English architect Michael Ventris. In this he was helped by John Chadwick, a Cambridge Classicist whose knowledge of early Greek was invaluable in the decipherment. That the language of Linear B is an early form of Greek is accepted by most scholars. His decipherment is considered even more remarkable than that of Champollion (Pharonic Egyptian), Rawlinson (Cuneiform) and Hrozny (Hittite) in that unlike the other three, Linear B had no bilingual texts.

In his excavations of the so-called Palace of Nestor at ancient Pylos – which is depicted in *The Iliad*—American archaeologist Carl Blegan unearthed a cache of about 600 tablets with Linear B inscriptions. He sent these to his student Emmett Bennett at the University of Cincinnati who after his service as a cryptanalyst in World War II started to analyze the tablets. This work, together with that done by classicist Alice Kober, was invaluable to Ventris in his breakthrough decipherment.

When Ventris began a systematic study of the Linear B tablets he already knew the language was a script of syllabograms, logograms, arithmetrograms, and metrograms. Evans in 1935 had already shown that the numeric system was a decimal one and Bennett (1950) had shown that the metrograms were organized in systems of multiples and submultiples.

FACTORS USED IN THE DECIPHERMENT

(1) Bennett's Classification

Emmett Bennett classified the thousands of characters into some 89 signs with a phonetic function (syllabograms) as distinguished from lone signs that were pictographic in character before numerals (logograms). The sign list is remarkably similar to the 87 characters accepted by most scholars today.

(2) Kober's Identifications

Alice Kober identified five sets of triplets, which suggested to her declensions as in Greek and Latin. From their context she deduced they were nouns, possibly place names or personal names. She also demonstrated that two Linear B words for "total" are masculine and feminine variants, the masculine variant appearing with the man logo and male animals and the female variant appearing with the female logo and female animals. The importance of this deduction was that the Indo-European languages are almost alone in this formation.

(3) The Cypriot Syllabary

The Cypriot Syllabary was finally deciphered by means of a bilingual that was written in both the Greek alphabetic script and the Cypriot Syllabary. The latter was found to be an open syllabary representing a dialect of Greek. Eight of the signs in the classical Cypriot Syllabary resembled those in Linear B. Ventris transferred the phonetic values of these onto his syllabic grid.

(4) Discovery of the Cache of Linear B Tablets in Pylos

The Linear B tablets found by Carl Blegan at Pylos did not contain names which were found only in Crete. Moreover, some of the names were names that survived into classical times. Ventris deemed them place names in Crete, which included Kober's triplets, for example Amnisos, the name of the port city of Knossos.

THE DECIPHERMENT BY VENTRIS

1. Ventris first calculated the frequency of different signs, as well as their frequency in different sign groups, in the initial, middle, and final positions. Statistical analysis of writing systems together with the frequency of the signs pointed to Linear B being a syllabary of the open type. Ventris deduced that signs found most frequently in the initial position were vowels by the logic that vowels in other positions in a syllabary would be subsumed within the syllables. Others that were found exclusively in the final position suggested a conjunction like "and."

2. Regular alternation among the syllabograms at the end of words suggested to Ventris inflection and grammatical case, as in the Latin

domi-ni (genitive singular) and domi-no (dative/ablative singular). He hypothesized that the alternating syllabograms had an identical consonant and a different vowel.

3. The syllabograms expressing different genders in the case of persons and animals as pointed out by Kober suggested to Ventris that syllables utilized for the same gender had different consonants but identical vowels, as in domi-ni and famu-li (i stands for nominative plural masculine although n and l are different consonants) as compared to domi-na and famu-la (nominative singular feminine) whereas different genders had the same consonant but different vowels as in famu-li (nominative plural masculine) and famu-la (nominative singular feminine).

4. Ventris noticed that the triplets identified by Kober appeared only in Crete and not in Pylos. He also knew there were place names in Crete that had survived into Classical times. Following a hunch that the triplets were place names in Crete, Ventris was able to work out the phonetic values of certain signs. The places identified in the triplets were Amnisos, Knossos, Tulissos, Phaistos, and Luktos. An example of a triplet whose phonetic values were worked out was that of Amnisos, the port of Knossos, and is as follows:

- Amnisos. Place name of the port city of Knossos.
- Amnisojo. Men of Amnisos.
- Amnisoja. Women of Amnisos.

Here the male-female variant can be clearly seen. Rather than declensions the suffixes turned out to be the name of towns with their ethnics.

However, patterns of declension did play a crucial part. An analysis showed that men's names inflected in six different forms, each with three different cases: nominative, genitive, and prepositional.

5. Ventris also took over the phonetic values of some of the signs of the Cypriot Syllabary that resembled the signs in Linear B.

6. Scribal variation where there were slightly different spellings suggested to Ventris there was a close relationship between the signs in one group and the sign that replaced it in another. For example, recognize and recognise.

7. He found plural forms useful as well.

There was, however, some skepticism on his part because of certain anomalies. For example, in Attic Greek the words for boy and girl are koros and kore, but in the Linear B script they were ko-wo and ko-wa. Chadwick, owing to his knowledge of early Greek and language change, was able to show that boy and girl in the archaic forms of Greek were korwos and korwa.

What finally emerged as a result of Ventris's analysis was that the underlying language of Linear B was an early form of Greek, Mycenaean Greek.

THE LINEAR B WRITING SYSTEM

Linear B signs are represented in Chart 5. The representations and naming of these signs have been standarised by a series of international colloquia which adopted a standard proposed primarily by Emmett L. Bennett, Jr.

CHART 5. The Linear B Symbols

The Linear B Syllabary (Signs shared with Linear A asterisked)

a	da	ja	ka	ma	na	pa	qa	ra	sa	ta	wa	za
e	de	je	ke	me	ne	pe	qe	re	se	te	we	ze
i	di		ki	mi	ni	pi	qi	ri	si	ti	wi	
o	do	jo	ko	mo	no	po	qo	ro	so	to	wo	zo
u	du	ju	ku	mu	nu	pu		ru	su	tu		zu

Linear B Signs for Sounds Not Found in the Hypothesized Linear A Syllabary with Pronunciation Underneath

a2 (ha), a3 (ai), au, dwe, dwo, nwa, pte, pu2 (phu), ra2 (rya), ra3 (rai), ro2 (ryo), ta2 (tya), twe, two

Undeciphered Signs

B018, B019, B022, B034, B047, B049, B056, B063, B064, B082, B083, B086

Some Linear B Logograms

People and Livestock
man, woman, ewe, ram, bull, cow, sow, boar, horse

Agricultural Products
wheat, barley, cyperus, olive oil, wine, spice, saffron

Military Equipment and Metals
bronze, gold, armor, helmet, spear, arrow, dart, chariot

Miscellaneous
cloth, wool, footstool, amphora, tripod, jug

Linear B is a logo-syllabic script composed of the following:

1. Syllabograms, 87 in number, some of them doubling as logograms.
2. Logograms, 170 in number representing persons, animals, objects and foodstuffs.
3. A numeric system of base 10 comprising 5 numerals (1, 10, 100, 1000, 10000).
4. Metrograms, comprising five symbols for weight and four symbols for volume.
5. Ligatures. Sometimes logograms and syllabograms combined to form ligatures.

Also in Linear B are a few rarely occurring signs whose phonetic values are unknown; they are transnumerated rather than transliterated.

Almost all the documents record different types of transactions, including inventories and assessments, as well as allocations. There is no evidence of historical, literary, legal, or other types of texts. However, the documents do give some indication of the political and religious structures of Mycenaean society as well as of certain cultural elements within it.

SPELLING CONVENTIONS OF LINEAR B

Linear B shares about 70% of its signs with Linear A from which it is derived. It appears that Linear B was adapted from the Linear A script to write an early form of Greek, Mycenaean Greek. Because Linear A was used to write a non-Greek language, it was ill adapted to fully reflect the phonetics, grammar, or spelling of Mycenaean Greek. In essence a limited number of syllabic signs had to represent a much greater number of sounds better represented phonetically by the letters of an alphabet. As a result orthographic simplification had to be made. Spelling conventions together with the invention of new signs were used to represent the sound patterns of Greek not found in the Linear A syllabary. For example:

1. Missing sounds in Linear B were represented by similar sounds

- p for [p], [b], and [ph]
- k for [k], [g], and [kh]
- t for [t] and [th]
- q for [kw] and [gw]
- r for [r] and [l]

In the Cypriot Syllabary the t sign stands not only for [t] and [th] but also for [d] as well, and r and l are disambiguated.

2. Spelling conventions were used to represent initial consonant clusters, ending consonants, and diphthongs, because syllables in Linear B usually represent Consonant Vowel (CV) syllables.

(a) In initial consonant clusters, all the consonants are written with syllables whose vowel agrees with the vowel of the final consonant, e.g. tri is written ti-ri.

(b) In ending consonant clusters, [k] and [p] are written similar to initial consonant clusters, whereas [l], [m], [n], [r], and [s] are not written. This is in contrast to the Cypriot script where all the syllables are written out. Final consonants in the Cypriot Syllabary are marked by a final silent e. For example, final consonants [n], [s], and [r] are noted by using ne, se, and re. The Cypriot script has two exceptions as discussed in the section on the Cypriot Syllabary.

(c) Diphthongs are similar to ending consonants in that some are written out and others are not. Diphthongs starting with [i] or [u] are written completely, sometimes with a vowel-only sign, sometimes with optional diphthong sign, or with a silent consonant. A diphthong ending in [i] usually omits the [i]. In Cypriot all the diphthongs were written out, the second part of the diphthong being written out with a vowel-only sign.

In addition to the standard syllabic grid of Linear B, certain signs representing diphthongs were invented, as shown in Chart 4.

3. Linear B did not distinguish between long and short vowels.

LOGOGRAMS

1. Some of the logograms are pictorial and some are symbolic.

2. Some syllabograms double as logograms. Categories are abbreviations and monograms. An example of the former is KU for ku-mi-no (cumin) and of the latter is the ligature ME+RI (meli for honey). However, the phonetic values of some logograms do not match the words they represent. Some believe these dual-role signs represent initial syllables of words of the underlying language. They are shown in Chart 6 and will be discussed in the section on Linear A.

From the missing sounds and additions to the standard grid certain inferences can be made about the structure of the underlying language of Linear A. From both Linear B and the Cypriot script, for example, we can infer that in the underlying language of Linear A there is no disambiguation between long and short vowels. We can also infer that the underlying language is composed of vowels and syllables but not of consonants or diphthongs, and that the following sounds are not represented: [b] [ph] [g] [kh] [kw] [gw] [ha] and either [th] or [t].

CHAPTER SIXTEEN

THE UNDERLYING LANGUAGE OF THE LINEAR A SCRIPT

THE SCRIPTS OF ANCIENT CRETE

Four different scripts were excavated in Crete: Cretan Hieroglyphics, the Phaistos Disc, Linear A, and Linear B. Because the Linear B script has already been discussed, a brief overview of the Cretan Hieroglyphs and the Phaistos Disc will be given before discussing the Linear A script. We will also discuss the so called "Eteo-Cretan language."

Cretan Hieroglyphics
Called Hieroglyphic by Evans because of its pictorial style, the writings date from about the 21st to the 16th century B.C. They were found at Knossos, Phaistos, Mallia, Petras, and Kato Symi on Crete, and on the Aegean islands of Samothrace and Kythera. About 350 inscriptions are extant, more than half inscribed on clay, the rest on ivory, stone, and metal seals. A few are painted on terra-cotta vases and stone objects.

Signs on the seals resemble natural objects including body parts, plants, animals, weapons, and ships, as well as more abstract symbols. Texts are short and formulaic and may have been used to impress owners' names on goods.

The clay tablets appear to be accounting and transaction records with numerical signs. The script seems to be logo-syllabic, with 96 syllabic signs, 10 of which double as logograms. Thirty-three logograms represent commercial goods, four numerical symbols, and nine fractions, which may be metrograms representing weights and measures.

About 20% of the Cretan Hieroglyphic signs are homomorphic with Linear A signs. In the Phaistos tablet (as opposed to the Phaistos Disc), which is illustrated in Chart Four, the transition from a hieroglyphic system to a Linear A accounting system can be clearly seen. Ideograms that stand for a word rather than a sound value occur only before numerals. The ideograms shown in the top section are those for wheat, oil, olives, and figs, and they occur before numerals and fractions. The quantities for each of the commodities appear to be 20 + 1/2. The words used for total and deficit in Linear A are "ku-ro" and "ki-ro." In Cretan Hieroglyphics they are "ku-ro" and "ki-ru." The two scripts have occasionally been found in the same archive.

The Phaistos Disc

The Phaistos Disc, the only one of its kind, was found during excavation at the palace of Phaistos and dates to the 2nd millennium B.C. It is 5.9 inches in diameter and covered on both sides with 45 hieroglyphic symbols. The archaeological context suggests that the disc dates to between 1850-1600 B.C., contemporaneous with Cretan Hieroglyphics and Linear A. The symbols were impressed rather than inscribed, and so the Phaistos Disc has been described as the world's first typewritten document. Controversy continues over whether it is an alphabetic, syllabic, or hieroglyphic script, over whether it is indigenous to Crete or an import, and over what language it represents. The script has weak connections with symbols inscribed on the Arkolochori Axe, a votive axe discovered in a cave dating to the same period. Evans postulated a link with Lycia, because one of the symbols depicted in the script resembled their rock tombs. The Phaistos Disc script remains undeciphered.

The Eteo-Cretan Language

The Eteo-Cretan language is attested to from the 7th to the 3rd century B.C. by inscriptions written in the alphabetic scripts of Archaic and Ionic Greek in the areas of Praisos and Dreros in eastern Crete. It was given the name "Eteo-Cretan," meaning "the true Cretans," by Domenico Comparetti, a Greek scholar in 1888. Homer mentions them along with Achaeans, Dorians, Kydones, and Pelasgians (*Odyssey* XIX, 176). The influx of different types of peoples following depopulation of the island after a destructive earthquake around 1300 B.C. has been discussed. Diodorus Siculus writes about a tradition pointing to the Eteo-Cretans as being the oldest autochthonous population of the island (Vol. 64, 1). The inscriptions in Praisos and Dreros show little evidence of the underlying language of Linear A. It is possible that the inscriptions may have represented the language of the original Neolithic population of Crete.

EVIDENCE FOR THE UNDERLYING LANGUAGE OF THE LINEAR A SCRIPT

Earlier in this study it was shown that Linear B was a syllabic script adapted from Linear A to write a dialect of Greek—Mycenaean Greek—but that spelling rules and additional symbols were needed because Linear A could not reproduce all the sounds of that language. This would rule out Greek as a contender for the Linear A language. In addition, Semitic scripts are primarily consonantal with a lack of vowels, not like Linear A and Linear B. Moreover, the Semitic languages have very few words in common with Linear A and no structural similarities to it, and so can be ruled out as a contender as well. Earlier in this study the link between the language of the Lycians, who had originally come from Crete, and the Elamite and Dravidian languages was shown. The link of the Linear A language to the Elamite and Dravidian languages will be explored in the following.

THE HYPOTHESIZED LINEAR A SYLLABARY

In this section we give clues to some of the words of the underlying language of Linear A. Earlier we showed how ill adapted the Akkadian cuneiform script was for writing the Elamite language and how heavily the Elamite language was influenced by the Mesopotamian and Achaemenid Persian languages. The modern Tamil alphabet rather than the Elamite script has therefore been chosen as the template for a discussion of the Hypothesized Linear A Syllabary and its links with the Elamo-Dravidian languages. The modern Tamil alphabet is really an alpha-syllabary rather than either a pure syllabary or an alphabet, because it has vowels, consonants, and syllables.

The Tamil alphabet is composed of 12 vowels and 18 consonants, which combine to form 216 syllables. The vowels, consonants, and syllables together form the 246 graphemes shown in Chart Six. When the long vowels, the pure consonants, and the diphthongs (shaded in gray)

THE UNDERLYING LANGUAGE OF THE LINEAR A SCRIPT

are removed from the Tamil alphabet what emerges gives clues to the Hypothesized Linear A Syllabary shown in Chart Seven.

Superimposition of the transliterated Linear B Signs on the Tamil alphabet give further clues about the Hypothesized Linear A Syllabary. The Hypothesized Linear A Syllabary was deduced from the following.

1. Linear B does not disambiguate between long and short vowels, and it is likely that Linear A also may not differentiate between the two.

2. The pure consonants are excluded in Linear B, so it is likely that Linear A has none.

3. Linear B created diphthongs so it is possible that Linear A had no diphthongs.

4. Linear B created certain letters, and used others from the Linear A script to double for sounds missing in the Mycenaean Greek language as shown earlier. These sounds are [g] [kh] [gw] [b] [ph] [kw]. These sounds are missing in the Tamil alphabet and possibly in the Hypothesized Linear A Syllabary.

5. Four out of the five nasal syllables of the "N" series are excluded in Linear B, but are probably present in Linear A as indicated by the Lycian connection. These are:

- Velar Nasal (ng)   ங
- Palatal Nasal (nj)   ஞ
- Retroflex Nasal (N)   ண
- Dental Nasal (n)   ந
- Alveolar nasal (n)   ன

CHART 6. The Tamil Alphabet

	க்	ங்	ச்	ஞ்	ட்	ண்	த்	ந்	ப்
	k	n	c	n	d	n	t	n	p
அ	க	ங	ச	ஞ	L	ண	த	ந	ப
a	ka	na	ça	na	da	na	ta	na	pa
ஆ	கா	ஙா	சா	ஞா	டா	ணா	தா	நா	பா
ā	kā	nā	çā	nā	dā	nā	tā	nā	pā
இ	கி	ஙி	சி	ஞி	டி	ணி	தி	நி	பி
i	ki	ni	çi	ni	di	ni	ti	ni	pi
ஈ	கீ	ஙீ	சீ	ஞீ	டீ	ணீ	தீ	நீ	பீ
ì	kì	nì	çì	nì	dì	nì	tì	nì	pì
உ	கு	ஙு	சு	ஞு	டு	ணு	து	நு	பு
u	ku	nu	çu	nu	du	nu	tu	nu	pu
ஊ	கூ	ஙூ	சூ	ஞூ	டூ	ணூ	தூ	நூ	பூ
ū	kū	nū	çū	nū	dū	nū	tū	nū	pū
எ	கெ	ஙெ	செ	ஞெ	டெ	ணெ	தெ	நெ	பெ
e	ke	ne	çe	ne	de	ne	te	ne	pe
ஏ	கே	ஙே	சே	ஞே	டே	ணே	தே	நே	பே
ē	kē	nē	çē	nē	dē	nē	tē	nē	pē
ஐ	கை	ஙை	சை	ஞை	டை	ணை	தை	நை	பை
ai	kai	nai	çai	nai	dai	nai	tai	nai	pai
ஒ	கொ	ஙொ	சொ	ஞொ	டொ	ணொ	தொ	நொ	பொ
o	ko	no	ço	no	do	no	to	no	po
ஓ	கோ	ஙோ	சோ	ஞோ	டோ	ணோ	தோ	நோ	போ
ō	kō	nō	çō	nō	dō	nō	tō	nō	pō
ஔ	கௌ	ஙௌ	சௌ	ஞௌ	டௌ	ணௌ	தௌ	நௌ	பௌ
au	kau	nau	çau	nau	dau	nau	tau	nau	pau

The grey areas indicate long vowels, consonants and diphthongs. As Linear B did not distinguish between long and short vowels, had orthographic

THE UNDERLYING LANGUAGE OF THE LINEAR A SCRIPT

ம்	ய்	ர்	ல்	வ்	ழ்	ள்	ற்	ன்
m	y	r	l	v	z	l	R	N
ம	ய	ர	ல	வ	ழ	ள	ற	ன
ma	ya	ra	la	va	za	la	Ra	Na
மா	யா	ரா	லா	வா	ழா	ளா	றா	னா
mā	yā	rā	tā	vā	zā	lā	Rā	Nā
மி	யி	ரி	லி	வி	ழி	ளி	றி	னி
mi	yi	ri	li	vi	zi	li	Ri	Ni
மீ	யீ	ரீ	லீ	வீ	ழீ	ளீ	றீ	னீ
mì	yì	rì	lì	vì	zì	lì	Rì	Nì
மு	யு	ரு	லு	வு	ழு	ளு	று	னு
mu	yu	ru	lu	vu	zu	lu	Ru	Nu
மூ	யூ	ரூ	லூ	வூ	ழூ	ளூ	றூ	னூ
mū	yū	rū	lū	vū	zū	lū	Rū	Nū
மெ	யெ	ரெ	லெ	வெ	ழெ	ளெ	றெ	னெ
me	ye	re	le	ve	ze	le	Re	Ne
மே	யே	ரே	லே	வே	ழே	ளே	றே	னே
mē	yē	rē	lē	vē	zē	lē	Rē	Nē
மை	யை	ரை	லை	வை	ழை	ளை	றை	னை
mai	yai	rai	lai	vai	zai	lai	Rai	Nai
மொ	யொ	ரொ	லொ	வொ	ழொ	ளொ	றொ	னொ
mo	yo	ro	lo	vo	zo	lo	Ro	No
மோ	யோ	ரோ	லோ	வோ	ழோ	ளோ	றோ	னோ
mō	yō	rō	lō	vō	zō	lō	Rō	Nō
மௌ	யௌ	ரௌ	லௌ	வௌ	ழௌ	ளௌ	றௌ	னௌ
ma	yau	rau	lau	vau	zau	lau	rau	Nau

rules for consonant clusters, and invented diphthongs, it can be hypothesized that the Linear A Syllabary did not have these three elements.

CHART 7. The Hypothesized Linear A Syllabary

அ	க	ங	ச	ஞ	L	ண	த	ந	U
a	ka	na	ça	na	da	na	ta	na	pa
இ	கி	ஙி	சி	ஞி	டி	ணி	தி	நி	பி
i	ki	ni	çi	ni	di	ni	ti	ni	pi
உ	கு	ஙு	சு	ஞு	டு	ணு	து	நு	பு
u	ku	nu	çu	nu	du	nu	tu	nu	pu
எ	கெ	ஙெ	செ	ஞெ	டெ	ணெ	தெ	நெ	பெ
e	ke	ne	çe	ne	de	ne	te	ne	pe
ஒ	கொ	ஙொ	சொ	ஞொ	டொ	ணொ	தொ	நொ	பொ
o	ko	no	ço	no	do	no	to	no	po

When the phonetic values of Linear B are transferred on to the Tamil Alpha-Syllabary, a hypothesized Linear A Syllabary emerges as shown above. It has 95 syllobograms. In addition to the 39 signs it has in common with Linear B, It has 20 of the four [n] series, 10 of the two [r] series, and 10 of the two [l] series, The phonetic values of 16 signs from the "Hypothesized Linear A syllabary" are not found in Linear B.They are shaded in grey in the chart as follows.

டொ	ணொ	மொ	வொ	யொ	லொ	பெ	மெ
Do	No	Mo	Vo	Yo	Lo	Pe	Me
வ	ல	யு	வு	லு	யி	லி	ல
Ve	Le	Yu	Vu	Lu	Yi	li	La

THE UNDERLYING LANGUAGE OF THE LINEAR A SCRIPT

ம	ய	ர	ல	வ	ழ	ன	ற	ண
ma	ya	ra	la	va	za	la	Ra	Na
மி	யி	ரி	லி	வி	ழி	னி	றி	ணி
mi	yi	ri	li	vi	zi	li	Ri	Ni
மு	யு	ரு	லு	வு	ழு	னு	று	ணு
mu	yu	ru	lu	vu	zu	lu	Ru	Nu
மெ	யெ	ரெ	லெ	வெ	ழெ	னெ	றெ	ணெ
me	ye	re	le	ve	ze	le	Re	Ne
மோ	யோ	ரோ	லோ	வோ	ழோ	னோ	றோ	ணோ
mo	yo	ro	lo	vo	zo	lo	Ro	No

There are 10 homomorphic signs common to both the Linear A and Linear B. However the phonetic values assigned to them in Linear B, are not found in the hypothesized Linear A syllabary. The 10 signs are as follows:

Pa2	Pu2	Ta2	Ra2	au	twe	Za	Zo	Ze	zu
16	29	66	76	85	87	17	20	74	79

There are 7 signs whose phonetic values are unidentified but are found in both Linear A and Linear B. They are transnumerated rather than transcribed.

22	34	47	49	56	82	86

It is possible that the 16 signs from the top section as well as one of the r's from the three r series taken to make "Ra2", were made to represent the other two sections making a total of 17.

At least four nasalized vowels were used in the Lycian language.

6. T was used for both [t] and [th] in Linear B. [th] but not [t] is present in the Tamil alphabet.

7. The Tamil Alphabet has three "R" signs for the fricatives.

- Flapped r ற
- Trilled r ர

Retroflex frictionless constituent [r] ழ (as in America). Represented in the Tamil alphabet and in the hypothesized Linear A syllabary by [z].

One of the r series was taken over by Linear B.

8. There were two "l" sounds, in the Tamil alphabet:

- Alveolar l ல
- Retroflex l ள

As there is no disambiguation between [r] and [l] in Linear B, neither of the "l" sounds were taken over by Linear B. Later it will be shown that there is no disambiguation between /l/, /r/, and /d/ in Linear A in certain cases.

9. When the phonetic values of Linear B are transferred on to the Tamil syllabary it can be seen that the "O", the "Y" (pronounced J), and the "V" series are underrepresented.

When the long vowels, the pure consonants, and the diphthongs are excluded from the Tamil alphabet, the Hypothesized Linear A Syllabary shown in Chart Seven emerges. It comprises 95 syllabograms, which accords well with the numbers of 90–97 allocated by most researchers in the field. I was able to count 95, plus an additional two signs that were of an ambiguous nature. Signs 328 and 371 stand alone and could be either syllables or logograms.

Transnumeration of the signs are from *Recueil des inscriptions en Linéaire A*, edited by Louis Godart and Jean-Pierre Olivier.

Some signs common to both Linear A and Linear B but which have no parallels in terms of phonetic values in the Hypothesized Linear A Syllabary or which have not been deciphered are categorized as follows:

1. Ten homomorphic signs are found in both Linear B and Linear A but are without parallels in the Hypothesized Linear A Syllabary in terms of phonetic values.

Pa2	Pu2	Ta2	Ra2	Au	Twe	Za	Zo	Ze	Zu
16	29	66	76	85	87	17	20	74	79

2. Seven undeciphered signs from Linear B that are also found in Linear A. They are transnumerated rather than transcribed, because their phonetic values are unknown.

22	34	47	49	56	82	86

3. Sixteen signs from the Hypothesized Linear A Syllabary not found in Linear B.

Do	No	Mo	Vo	Yo	Lo	Pe	Me

வெ	லெ	யு	வு	லு	யி	லி	லா
Ve	Le	Yu	Vu	Lu	Yi	Li	La

It is possible that the 16 signs in Category 3 were used for 16 of the total of 17 signs in Categories 1 and 2 and that "Ra2" was taken from one of the other "R" series in the Hypothesized Linear A Syllabary.

The reasons for reconstructing the Hypothesized Linear A syllabary was as follows:

1. The number of syllables in the Linear A tablets amounted to roughly between 90 and 97 according to different researchers. This accorded well with the number 95 reached.

2. The symbol for "Do" in Linear B was not shared with Linear A, although the symbol for "Ro" was. Also the other symbols in the D series "Da", "De", "Di", and "Du", are. Because of the lack of disambiguation of /r/, /l/, and /d/ shown below it strengthens the case that "Do" was taken to represent "Ro" This is discussed on the section on the transaction signs.

3. Sixteen signs from the Hypothesized Linear A Syllabary did not have corresponding phonological values in the Linear B Syllabary but were represented in both scripts. Ten of them were taken to represent sounds in Mycenaean Greek. Seven were undeciphered. It is possible that the sixteen signs in the Hypothesized Linear A Syllabary with no corresponding phonological values in the Linear B syllabary may have been used. There are three of the "R" series as shown. "Ra2" may have been taken from one of the alternate "R" series.

THE UNDERLYING LANGUAGE OF THE LINEAR A SCRIPT

THE LINEAR A SCRIPT

Linear A is one of the scripts excavated by Arthur Evans in Crete. Linear A of the time of the First Palace Period was found almost exclusively at Phaistos (20th–17th centuries B.C.). Linear A of the time of the Second Palace Period was found throughout Crete—though mostly in the minor palace of Hagia Triada—and on the Aegean Islands of Kea, Melos, Thera, and Samothrace, as well as in Miletus in Asia Minor, and rarely on the Greek Mainland (17th–13th centuries B.C.).

There are about 1,500 inscriptions in Linear A, far less than the 6,000 in Linear B. And unfortunately many of the Linear A tablets are damaged and illegible, making decipherment that much harder. About 90% of the inscriptions are engraved on clay tablets, bars, roundels and sealings, while the rest are engraved on stone or clay vases, gold and silver pins and rings, and on stone, metal, terra cotta, and ivory objects. Inscriptions on clay vases are sometimes painted.

Like Linear B, Linear A is a logo-syllabic script with logograms corresponding to words, and syllabograms corresponding to syllables. There are also signs for numbers as well as fractional signs used for the measurement of weights and volumes. Together they comprise what are known as the simple signs. Often syllabograms, logograms, and the symbols for fractions combine among themselves forming ligatures or complex signs.

Researchers place the number of syllabograms between 90 and 97. Statistically they are of the open type, that is, CV. The Hypothesized Linear A Syllabary has 95. Some syllabograms occur in isolation and are termed transaction signs by convention, because they register the type and nature of the transaction being made. Some of the syllabograms double as logograms.

About 50 logograms have been identified; they represent men, animals, goods, and objects. There are four signs for the numbers 1,10,100, and 1000, and 17 signs for fractions used for the measurement of weights and volumes. These 17 signs for fractions combine among themselves to form 30 ligatures. The Linear A syllabograms that are shared with Linear B are asterisked in Chart Five. The rest are shown in Chart Eight.

RATIONALE FOR THE TRANSLITERATION OF THE PHONETIC VALUES OF LINEAR B SCRIPT ON TO THE LINEAR A SCRIPT.

About 69 of the Linear A and Linear B signs are homomorphic. The rationale for transliterating the phonetic values of Linear B on to Linear A is discussed below.

1. The method used by Ventris in deciphering Linear B by using the triplets identified by Kober offers a clue. Words of some length differing in one or two signs may be variant spelling of the same word, or may be an indication of inflection. Examples in the very limited material of Linear A are:

(a) a-sa-ra-me
 ja-sa-sa-ra-me
 ja-sa sa ra ma-na
(b) un-aru-ka-na-si
 un-aru-ka-na-ti
(c) su-ki-ri-ta
 su-ki-ri-te-i-ja

(d) pi-ta-ka-se

   pi-ta-ke-si

(e) ku-do-ni

   kau-do-ni

The sounds are very similar with slight variation. There is a similar alternation in Linear B.

2. When Linear A sign groups transliterated with Linear B values are compared with sign groups of known value in Linear B, a number of doublets emerge as follows.

Linear A	*Linear B*
a-ma-ra-tu	a-ma-ru-ta-o
di-de-ru	di-de-ro
di-ka-tu	di-ka-to-jo
pa-ra-tu	pa-ra-to
ta-pa-du	ta-pa-da-no

The words selected have parallels up to the third consonant, and end in "u" in Linear A and in "o" in Linear B. This is not so in all cases. However, an analysis shows that the frequency of the vowel "u" at the end of words is much higher in Linear A than in Linear B, and the frequency of the vowel "o" is much lower.

It is in proper nouns and in place names that there is overlap in languages, suggesting that the above doublets refer to the two of them.

CIVILIZATIONS OF THE UNCONSCIOUS

CHART 8. Possible Linear A syllables not shared with Linear B

| 301 | 304 | 305 | 306 | 307 | 308 | 310 | 311 | 312 | 315 | 317 | 319 | 321 | 322 | 323 |

| 324 | 325 | 327 | 329 | 331 | 332 | 333 | 342 | 345 | 349 | 353 | 354 | 355 | 357 | 362 |

Some Linear A Logograms

People and Livestock

man/woman · man · bovines · bull · goat · pig · sheep

Agricultural Products

wheat · barley · cyperus · figs · olives · oil · wine

Some Linear B syllables which double up as logograms

	Flax	Ox	Sheep	Figs
Commodity				
Phonetic Value of Logogram in Linear B	Sa	Mu	Qi	Ni
Mycenaean Greek word	Linon	Gwous	Owis	Sukon
Tamil word	Sanam	Madu	Kori	Ni (from Kikini)

Numerals, weights and measures in Linear B

Numerals: 1, 10, 100, 1000, 10,000

Weights: 12 ? = 1, 4 = 1, 30 ? = 1

Measures:
Dry: 6 = 1, 10 = 1 unit
Wet: 4 = 1, 6 = 1, 3 = 1 unit

Numerals Weights and measures in Linear A

Numerals: 1, 10, 100, 1000

THE UNDERLYING LANGUAGE OF THE LINEAR A SCRIPT

Category One (Aliquots of eighths)	1/8	2/8 (1/4)	3/8	4/8 (1/2)	5/8	6/8 (3/4)
Category Two (Aliquots of twelfths)	1/12	1/6	2/6 (1/3)	3/6 (1/2)	4/6 (2/3)	5/6

Example HT 123 + 124

	logogram	number	logogram	number	deficit	number
ki-ta-i	olive	31	308	8E	ki-do	1X
pu-vi-na	olive	31J	308	8JE	ki-do	X
sa-ru	olive	16	308	4A	ki-do	JE
da-tu	olive	15	308	4E	ki-do	JE
ku-do	olive	93J	308		ki-do	6
ku-do				25H	ki-do	

Fractions	J	E	A	H	X	JE
Values Assigned	1/2	1/4	1/12	1/3	1/6	3/4

	logogram	number	logogram	number	deficit	number
ki-ta-i	olive	31	308	8 1/4	ki-do	1 1/6
pu-vi-na	olive	31J	308	8 3/4	ki-do	1/6
sa-ru	olive	16	308	4 1/2	ki-do	3/4
da-tu	olive	15	308	4 1/4	ki-do	3/4
ku-do	olive	93J	308		ki-do	6
ku-do				25 1/3	ki-do	8 2/3?

Category Three

Category Four

3. To rule out coincidences, however, Harvard doctoral student David Packard set out to conduct a rigorous scientific analysis of the Linear A inscriptions. He wanted to show that the phonetic values of Linear B and no other set of values, when substituted in Linear A, would produce Linear A/Linear B doublets. He constructed nine false decipherments in which no Linear A sign took the same value in any two of the false decipherments, while making allowances for the fact that the frequency of Linear A signs differed, and that the signs were position-dependent. When he used a computer to apply his nine decipherments to the Linear A corpus, the results were statistically significant. The Linear B values produced doublets more frequently than in his other decipherments, showing the applicability of Linear A values to Linear B. Also, the overlap in place names and personal names were confined to Crete. He did, however, caution that his conclusions did not possess any special validity just because a computer was involved.

4. It must be kept in mind that even though many signs in Linear A and Linear B appear to be morphologically similar, they may have different phonetic values. An example of this is the Cyrillic Alphabet which was derived from the Roman alphabet in the 9th century A.D. The Cyrillic letters B, C, P, and X stand for V, S, R and H. Also, as shown earlier in a discussion of the Hypothesized Linear A Syllabary, some of the signs of Linear A may have been taken over by Linear B and given different phonetic values.

THE LACK OF DISAMBIGUATION OF /R/, /L/, AND /D/

In his book *The Mycenaean World*, John Chadwick pointed out that the title "Potnia" (mistress or lady) is an inherited Greek title used of queens. Potnia is often accompanied by epithets like "Aswia" (of Asia), "Iqeja" (of horses), and "Wanosoi" or "Dipisijoi," which are places or festivals characterizing her—compare the Roman Catholic use of the term "Our Lady of Lourdes." It is apparent that the word "Potnia" does not stand alone. The inscription on Knossos tablet Gg 702 is transliterated as Da-pu-ri-to-jo Po-ti-ni-ja. According to Chadwick the first word bears a strong resemblance to Laburinthos (labyrinth) in that, in the borrowing of pre-Hellenic words, /d/ and /l/ were sometimes confused. Also the spelling conventions used in Linear B. discussed earlier should be noted. While Potnia is a Greek word, Laburinthos is a pre-hellenic borrowing as the –nthos suffix shows. A parallel case was that of Oluseus, which in Greek dialects became Odusseus. Latin borrowed the name making it Ulysses or Ulixes. This l/d ambivalence is documented in other ancient languages of the area as well (Huebeck, 1957).

In addition, one difference between Cuneiform Luwian and Hieroglyphic Luwian is that the latter shows frequent "Rhotacism," Rho pertaining to the Greek letter of the same name. That is, Rho replaces /d/ and often /l/ with /r/. Overall it is seen that /r/, /l/, and /d/ are not disambiguated in Ancient Greek and in other languages of the area of the eastern Mediterranean or Anatolia. It can also be seen that the /l/ series elements are not represented in the Linear B syllabary because of the lack of r/l disambiguation. The sign "do" in Linear B is one of the signs not taken over from the Hypothesized Linear A Syllabary, although the rest of the "d" series elements are (see Chart Seven). They created a sign for "do". Due to the lack of /r/, /l/, and /d/ disambiguation it is likely that the "do" of the Hypothesized Linear A Syllabary was taken over to represent "ro" in Linear B, and a new symbol was created for "do" in the script.

DECODING THE LINEAR A SCRIPT

The dictionaries used for Elamite were primarily *Elamisches Worterbüch* by Hinz and Koch, and *Persepolis Fortification Tablets* by Hallock; *A Comprehensive Tamil and English Dictionary* by Winslow and Winslow's *English Tamil Dictionary* were used for Tamil.

1. THE TRANSACTION SIGNS

As discussed earlier, transaction signs register the type and nature of the transaction being made. In the Linear A tablets, these appear to deal with allocations and assessments. When Linear B values are transliterated onto Linear A, there are words paralleled by words in Linear B indicating "Total," "Grand Total," and "Deficit." The transliterated words in Linear A are "Kuro," "Potokuro," and "Kiro." When "do" is substituted for "ro," for reasons discussed earlier, the transaction signs that emerge are "Kudo," "Potokudo," and "Kido."

In Tamil, "Kudu" means aggregate, "Potokudu" bundled aggregate, and "Kidai" means "deficit" or "to be obtained." As discussed earlier, the word for deficit in the Cretan Hieroglyphics is "kidu." In Elamite the word means "outside" and could indicate "missing." The transaction sign "Te" or "The" most probably stands for "tha," meaning "give" in Tamil.

"Kuda" in HT 122 means "cavity" or "missing" in Tamil. When the total of 31+ 65 is added to the missing number of 1 (Kuda) the grand total (Potokudo) of 97 is reached.

HT 12 lists various rations meted out. At the bottom, which would have the word "Kudo" or "Kidu," there is the word "Da-I." In Elamite the word means "under" and could refer to a deficit.

The transaction signs with the exception of "tha" are clearly seen in Chart Nine. They are asterisked.

- "Kudu" (செடு) = Aggregate
- "Potokudu" (பொட்டணம் = Bundle) = Bundled Aggregate
- "Kidai" (கிடை) = To be obtained
- "Tha" (தா) = Give
- "Kuda" (குபா) = Cavity
- "Dai" (டை) = Under or Deficit in Elamite

They are all asterisked in HT 122 except for "Dai" and are shown in Chart Nine.

2. THE NUMERICAL AND METRICAL SYSTEM

(a) The Numerical System

Evans established that the numerical system of Linear A was basically the same as that of Linear B, except that an alternate sign for 10, a heavy dot was used as well. It is shown in Chart Eight.

It is a decimal system with numbers for 1, 10, 100, and 1000.

(b) The Metrical System.

Bennett carried out a frequency analysis of the signs following

CHART 9. HT122 The Transaction Signs

	logogram	number
u-de-za		2
		2
da-si-118		2
pa-[-]		
]-di		1
te-ki		2
qa-310-i		3
ja-mi-da-re		1
si-da-re		1
324-di-ra		1
pa-de		1
ku-pa3-nu		1
pa-ta-ne		1
306-tu		1
]du		1
ku-pa3-nu		1
da-ri-da		1
ku-do*		31
ku-da*		1
je-di	346-vir	
]306-ki-ta2		7
]a-ra-ju-u-de-za		2
qa-qa-ru		2
	di	2
da-re		2
Ku-do*		65
po-to-ku-do*		97

logograms in Linear A and showed that they were fractional numerals, not the decimal system used in Linear B. At the same time he pointed out that one of the difficulties in assigning values to the numerical signs in Linear A was the scarcity of well-preserved tablets in which fractional signs as well as their summations appeared. He also postulated that weights and liquid measures were not distinguished. The Mycenaeans used a decimal system for weights and measures and distinguished between weights as well as volumes for dry and liquid measures. A study of the Mycenaean metric system, however, shows certain resemblances in the signs between the two metric systems. Because of the ligature system of Linear A, the difference between fractional values for liquids and weights is not clear cut.

The fractional values of Linear A can be placed into four categories, depending on their frequency values, placement in monograms, morphological similarities, and whether they were used to measure weights or volumes. The Mycenaean system for weights and volumes is given in Chart Eight and the similarities between the two systems are pointed out. At this stage because of the lack of summations in the Linear A tablets, the fractional values as well as the categories to which I have assigned them are speculative.

Chart Eight shows the different categories.

Category 1. This remains the same as that of Bennett's except that the monograms are made more explicit. They are fractions of eighths.

Category 2. These are fractions of twelfths.

The following tablets are taken to show the fractional values that I have assigned. HT stands for Hagia Triada.

CIVILIZATIONS OF THE UNCONSCIOUS

HT 123+124

	Logogram	Number	Logogram	Number	Deficit	Number
1. Ki-Ta-I	Olives	31	308	8E	Ki-Do	1X
2. Pu-Vi-Na	Olives	31J	308	8JE	Ki-Do	X
3. Sa-Ru	Olives	16	308	4A	Ki-Do	JE
4. Da-Tu	Olives	15	330	4E	Ki-Do	JE
5. Ku-Do	Olives	93J	308		Ki-Do	6
6. Ku-Do				25H	Ki-Do	

Fractions	J	E	A	H	X	JE
Values Assigned	1/2	1/4	1/12	1/3	1/6	3/4
or	6/12	3/12	1/12	4/12	2/12	3/12

The fractional values for the letters are assigned in HT 123+124 as follows.

	Logogram	Number	Logogram	Number	Deficit	Number
1. ki-Ta-I	Olive	31	308	8 1/4	Ki-Do	1 1/6
2. Pu-Vin	Olive	31 1/2	308	8 3/4	Ki-Do	1/6
3. Sa-Ru	Olive	16	308	4 1/12	Ki-Do	3/4
4. Da-Tu	Olive	15	308	4 1/4	Ki-Do	3/4
5. Ku-Do	Olive	93 1/2	308		Ki-Do	6
6. Ku-Do				25 1/3	Ki-Do	8 2/3?

(Not shown in tablet)

Using the fractional values that I have assigned for Category 2 shown in Chart Eight, the total for the olives of 93 J (line 5) is correct. The value assigned for "J" then becomes 1/2. The total for the logogram "308" is 25 H (line 6), which makes the value assigned to "H" "1/3" and the value assigned to line 3 for A 1/12th. The total for the deficits is not shown in the tablet because it has been broken off. The total deficit cannot be 6, the value assigned by some researchers, because all the fractional values of the deficits do not and cannot add up to 6. So the number 6 appears to be the deficit for line 5 of logogram "308." The total would then add up to 8, + 2/3 which is not shown on the tablet because the end is broken off. There is some overlap in the values of Category 1 and Category 2 and they may have been used to measure different types of commodities.

Category 3. These are measurements of volume but no values are given. The liquid measures in Linear B are given above the Linear A fractional values in Category 3 in Chart Eight. The cup measure is upright not horizontal, and the sign morphologically similar to "p" has been rotated. In eight out of the nine tablets in which the upright cup appears, it is associated with cyperus. Chadwick says that the word probably refers to *cyperus rotundus*, an aromatic plant used for the making of perfumed oil. Using volume as a measure for this makes sense. However, cyperus also indicates a grass used as fodder in other contexts. It is possible that this grass was also used for making a perfumed oil. No numeric values are assigned.

Category 4. In this, the Mina and the double Mina and the quadruple Mina are used for the measurement of weight. Mina is the word used by the Greeks. Again no numeric values are given.

3. LINEAR A PHONETIC VALUES ASSIGNED TO SOME LOGOGRAMS THAT WERE DISCUSSED EARLIER

(a) HT 88 has the ideogram for figs followed by Kikina, which was thought to refer to a variety of figs. In Tamil the word "Kikini" refers to a specific type of "plant" but could have been specifically referring to the fig plant because of the association to the word figs. Tablet (Gv 862) in Linear B refers to 1770 fig trees. It is possible that Kikina may refer to fig trees rather than a variety of figs. This was one of the commodities used extensively by the Mycenaeans as well as by the Cretans.

(b) As discussed earlier on the section on Linear B, some Linear B syllabograms double as logograms. However, when the phonetic value of these logograms is compared with the Mycenaean Greek word they represent, they do not represent the first syllable of the Greek word. For example, the syllable "Sa" is used to represent flax, but the Mycenaean word for flax is "Linon." Some believe these dual role signs represent the initial syllables of words in the underlying language of Linear A, representing the logogram. In fact, there is a match for some of the signs.

Commodity	Flax	Ox	Sheep	Figs
	𐘀	𐘁	𐘂	𐘃
Phonetic Value of Logogram	Sa	Mu	Qi	Ni
Mycenaean Greek Word	linon	Gwous	Owis	Sukon
Tamil Word	Sanam	Madu	Kori	Ni
				(from Kiki-ni)

4. CLASSIFICATION OF THE LINEAR A TABLETS

Bennett was able to make an accurate classification of Linear B tablets from Pylos and later of the Knossos tablets according to their apparent subject matter. His criteria included recurrent formulaic phrases and ideograms, as well as the identification of the different scribal hands of those who inscribed the tablets. However, the classificatory system of the Linear B cannot be easily transposed on to Linear A. The two scripts mirror aspects of two very different cultures. Mycenaean society was essentially a militaristic society, heavily dependent on slaves for its economy, and imbued with both social stratification and private ownership of land. The Linear B documents show not only the distribution of rations to occupational groups and slaves, but also inventories of the weapons of war and of land tenure. By contrast, archaeological evidence points to Crete being overall an egalitarian society with communal land holding and with no overt evidence of land tenure. In addition, ancient Crete had an extensive maritime fleet for trade as well as for defense. Accordingly, some of the tablets reflect the manning and equipping of ships. The Linear B tablets list the following.

1. Personnel, in terms of place, occupation, ethnicity (in the case of slaves), and the rations meted out to them.
2. Inventories of cattle, wool and textiles, aromatics and unguents, household effects, metals, and military equipment.
3. Ritual offerings to deities.
4. Land Tenure

A broad classification of the Linear A documents would be:

1. Texts dealing with the military and with economic segments of society, inscribed mainly on clay tablets and roundels.
2. Religious inscriptions mainly from the peak sanctuaries. They are inscribed on stone vases (libation tables), clay vases, terra-cotta figurines, and metal objects which came from sanctuaries.
3. Other inscriptions, mainly inscribed on rings and pins of precious metals.

Like Linear B, 80% of the lists in Linear A comprise place names or personal names. Because of the overlap in languages of this category, where Linear B indicates a place name replicated in Linear A, the Linear A word is presumed to be a place name as well. An example of a place name found in both Linear A and Linear B is Paito (Phaistos). Sometimes in Linear B a place name could be a personal name as well. That this is so in Linear A as well could not be verified. Nevertheless, Linear A names appear to identify assessments and allocations meted out to them.

Place Names in Linear A	*Place Names in Linear B*
Akaru	Akareute
Aparane	Apareu
Asijaka	Asijatija
Dataro	Dataramo
Dikatu	Dikatade
Kudoni	Kudonija
Samaro	Samarade
Sukiriteseja	Sukiritajo

Ethnic Names in Linear A	*Linear B Equivalents*
Raride	Raridija
Kasaru	Kasaro
Dideru	Dideru

1. TEXTS DEALING WITH THE MILITARY AND ECONOMIC SEGMENTS OF SOCIETY

(a) The equipment of ships

Being primarily a nation with settlements and spheres of influence in the Aegean region, as well as one dependent heavily on a navy for defense and trade, the building and manning of ships together with the distribution of equipment and commodities to ships was an important part of the Cretan economy. This is seen in tablets HT 6, HT 94, HT 102, and HT 105, where there are indications of the equipping of ships with personnel and provisions. The inscriptions all have the heading "Kapa" and three of them have the word "Sara." Kapal in Tamil means ship (கப்பல்) and the word "Sarangu" in Tamil means overseer of boatmen (சரங்கு). In Elamite "Sara" has the meaning supervisor.

In all of the tablets there are different kinds of the man logo, or of commodities. For example, in HT 94 there are two different kinds of the man logo followed by whole numbers (whole numbers usually refer to persons, livestock, or certain objects like vases although in some instances they can also refer to agricultural products).The word "Sara" is followed by logos for commodities such as figs and cyperus where fractions are included. HT 94 also has the boat logo AB 86, which may have been needed for docking in the harbors. The tablet HT 94 is shown in Chart Ten.

In HT 105 the numbers with the man logo total over 400. Overall the tablets might be showing the different types of personnel needed to man the ships, together with the equipment and provisions needed for the voyage. The reverse side has "kido" (கிடோ) "deficit" with what appear to be place names followed by the number one. This could possibly refer to regions where ships have to be built, or to shipbuilders.

CHART 10. The Manning and Equipment of Ships

	logogram	number	fraction
Ka-pa*	vir	62	
	86	20	
	ti+ A (523)	7	
	vir=313b (57	18	
	ta	4	
ku-ro*		110	
sa-ra*	303	5	
	fic	3	H
		2	
	318-306	11	
	303		D D
	fic		D D
		14	J
	fic		D
ki-do*			
tuma		1	
pa-ta-ne		1	
de-di		1	
ke-ki-ru		1	
sa-ru		1	
kuro*		5	

Fighting Units

HT 27 tinita	307	木	vir	90
KH 9	307	木	vir	
HT 127 kuro	307	木	vir	156
HT 85	638r	木木	vir	
HT 97 karu	638	木木	vir	82

(b) Fighting units?

HT 27, KH 9, HT 127, HT 97, and HT 85 appear to deal with military fighting units.

(i) HT 27, KH 9, and HT 127 have the logo 307. HT27 and KH9 are associated with the man logo. HT127 has the total "Kudo" followed by the logo 307.

HT 27 is headed by TI-NI-TA followed by a man logo attached to logo 307. Thinicam (திணிகம்) in Tamil means battle/fight and logo 307 associated with a man logo appears to be related to fighting units.

HT 127 has the logo "307" (the possible fighting units) totaled as 156. This is followed by more logograms, one of them of a man logo totaling 135. The two totals add up to 292 which is the correct total. The tablets showing the fighting units are depicted on Chart Ten.

(ii) HT 97 and HT 85 have the logo 638, and are associated with different man logos. The logo 638 appears to be a doubling of logo 307.

HT 97 has KA-RU followed by logo 638 which appears to duplicate logo 307. Logo 307 and logo 638 may indicate fighting units like divisions, brigades, and battalions. HT 85 too has the logo 638 followed by a man logo.

(c) Allocations and Inventories

HT 114, HT 121, and HT 129 have the name "Kirita" with "Sara" as a subheading in two of them. "Kirita" (கிரீடா) refers to a crowned king. Sara may not be restricted to the role of overseer of boatmen, but may refer to overseer in general, as the Elamite meaning indicates. Succeeding names may refer to other officials of the king.

HT 21 has Pitakase followed by logograms for agricultural products. HT 87 has Pitakesi together with possible names of other officials followed by the number I. Pitakan (பிடகன்) in Tamil means physician.

(d) Livestock documents

HT 9 and HT 11 have Ka 305 and the Ka ideogram respectively.m They are both followed by whole numbers which usually refer to livestock when they do not refer to personnel. Ka could stand for Kalai, (காளை) bulls. As discussed earlier, bulls played an important part in Cretan ritual and culture.

(e) Agricultural documents

Agricultural documents comprise the majority of documents from the different sites of Crete. Agricultural ideograms include figs, olives, wheat, barley, olive oil, wine, and cyperus. Examples are HT 27, HT89, HT94, and HT 100.

(f) Miscellaneous

These include cloth, different kinds of pots, and household effects. Examples are HT 16 and HT 20 which have a pictorial ideogram for an upright loom. HT 31 presents seven different ideograms for pots.

(g) Months of the year

There are references in some of the documents to months of year. HT 43 refers to Masilu (மசிலு), February and most of March. HT 117 and HT 87 refer to Makarita (மக்கம்). Makam refers to the month of February or 10th lunar month.

2. RELIGIOUS INSCRIPTIONS

(1) Religious Inscriptions occur on stone vases, also called libation tables. They were found mostly at the sanctuaries of Mounts Iouktas, Dikte, and Ida, and to a lesser extent at those of Petsophas, Psychro, Symi, Viannou, Troullos, and Vrysinas, They were also found less frequently in urban contexts such as Apodolou, Knossos, Nerokouru, Palaikastro, Prassa, and Kastri in Kythera. Many of these inscriptions are repetitively formulaic. They are also fragmentary owing to the poor condition of the libation tables. Tables having sections of the libation texts to a lesser or greater amount are the following: AP Apodoulou, IO Iouktas, KN Knossos, KO Kophinas, MA Malia, PK Palaikastro, PL Platonos, SY Syme, TL Tyllisos, and ZA Zakros.

(Note: Za means the inscription is on a stone vessel; Zb on a pot; Zc an inked inscription; Zd a mark of graffito; Ze on architecture; Zf on a metal object; and Zg on stone.)

- AP Za 1 and 2
- IO Za 2.1-2, 2.2, 4, 6, 7, and 9 and 10
- KN Za 10, 17, 18, 19, KN Zc 7, KN Ze 44
- KO Za 1 and 3
- MA Zb 8
- PK Za 4, 8, 9, 11, 12, 14, 15, 17, and 18
- PL Zf 1.1
- SY Za 1, 2, and 3
- TL Za1
- ZA Zb 3

One relatively intact is PK Za 11 as shown below. Undeciphered syllables are given their numerical number.

(Note: [means text broken off at the left;] means text broken off at the right; and [ ] means an erased but legible sign.)

A-TA-I-301-WA E. A-DI-KI-TE-TE.]-RE. PI-TE-RI. A-KO-A-NE. A-SA-SA-RA-ME U-NA-RU-KA-NA-TI. I-PI-NA-MI-NA. SI-RU [ ]. I-NA-JA-PA-QA.

Missing sections have been reconstructed from other inscriptions having similar or almost similar formulas. The final text appears to be as follows.

A-TA-I 301-WA-E (JA). A-DI-KI-TE-TE (TU)
]RE. PI-TE-RI. A-KO-A-NE.
A (JA)-SA-SA-RA-ME (MA-NA). U-NA-RU-KA-NA-TI (SI)
I-PI-NA-(MA)- MI-NA . SI-RU-TE. I-NA-JA-PA-QA.

The syllables in parentheses indicate alternate variants in other inscriptions for the last syllable or the last two syllables.

Transliteration and translation.

- "A" an invocation
- "Tai" "Thai" (தாய் = Mother) (Tamil syllable /t/ standing for /th/ and thai is the Tamil word for mother).
- "Wa" (வா = Come) (Tamil word)
- "Dikiitete" (டிகிடேடே = of Mount Dikite) ("e" is third person animate singular possessive suffix in Elamite)
- "Piteri" Personal names of a couple ? (possibly supplicants)

- "Akoane"
- (i) "Asasarame", "jasasarame"

  (யசசாலை jasasalai = a sacrificial hall in Tamil)

  (r(a) is third person derivational suffix of animates indicating the agent noun e.g., "makers" in Elamite).

  (The inanimate "me" indicates the abstract of sacrificer, i.e. "sacrifice" in Elamite)

- (ii) "Asasaramana", "jasamanan"

  (யசமானன் = the offerer of a sacrifice in Tamil)

  ("na" indicates possession in Elamite – thus the sacrifice of)

- "Unaru" (உணரு = to possess full and perfect knowledge in Tamil)
- "Kanati" (கண் kan = Tamil word for eyes) ("na" indicates possession and "ti" occurs in subordinate clauses in Elamite)
- "Ipinamina" (பிணி pini means affliction or disease in Tamil, ?sterility) ("na" indicates possession in Elamite)
- "Sirute" (சிருட்டி = the creating deity in Tamil)
- "Inajapaqa" (யாபணாடம் japanadam = things longed for by the pregnant women in Tamil)

Possible translation

O mother of Mount Dikte, Piteri and Akoane , makers of the sacrifice, implore you to come. We have an affliction (sterility?) and implore you, creating and all-seeing deity, possessor of perfect knowledge, to give us a child.

As discussed earlier, in Cretan and Mycenaean religion, Artemis—also called Eileithya—was connected with the tree cult and the sacred bough that conveyed life and fertility. She also helped in childbirth and fostered small children and young animals, and she was worshipped in the "Cave of Eileithya."

(2) The following tables refer to Mount Ida instead of Mount Dikte. KO. Za 1, (KO for Kophinas); IO. Za 2, (IO for Iouktas); SY. Za 1, (SY for Syme); PK. Za 18, and PK. Za 17, (PK for Palaikastro).

The table on PK.Za 1 refers to Setoija, a place name.

(3) A stone ladle from Kythera KY. Za2 refers to another goddess Da-ma-te (Demeter)

AR. Zf 1, a gold ax, and AR. Zf, 2 a silver ax, both from Arkalokhori refer to I-Da-ma te.

3. OTHER INSCRIPTIONS

These are some of the relatively long inscriptions found on objects other than those of the sacrificial tables. Ones on jewelry are on a gold pin from Crete, CR Zf 1; a gold ring from Knossos, KN Zf 13; a silver pin from Knossos, KN Zf 31; and a silver hairpin from Arkhanes, ARKH Zf 9. These inscriptions are hard to decipher. For example KN Zf 13 has no dividers, and none of them are repetitively formulaic.

Other inscriptions are IO Za5 on a stone lamp; KN Zc 6, an inked inscription in the interior of a conical cup; and KO Zf 2 on a bronze mesomphalos.

The evidence gathered not only from an analysis of the Linear A script, but also from the links between the ancient Lycian language with both the Elamite language and the Dravidian language of Tamil, point to the underlying language of Linear A being an

Elamo-Dravidian language. While the lexicon is mostly that of the Tamil language, the morphology is predominantly Elamite. As some of the ancient peoples speaking an early form of Tamil/Elamite inhabiting the area of the Eastern Persian Plateau and possibly the southern parts of ancient Central Asia moved westward possibly owing to earthquakes or climatic changes, their dialects were modified by the languages of the surrounding people. This is most clearly seen in the case of the Elamites. The conquest by adjoining Mesopotamians, as well as the imposition of their language and scripts, especially by the Akkadians, on the Elamites led to changes in the lexicon, but not the morphology of the Elamite language.

CONCLUSION

THE LINK BETWEEN ANCIENT CRETE, ANCIENT CYPRUS, ANCIENT LYCIA, ANCIENT ELAM, AND THE INDUS VALLEY CIVILIZATION

Evidence gathered from the partial decipherment of the Linear A script points to its underlying language being Elamo-Dravidian. Of the Dravidian language family, Tamil appears to be the one used in the script of ancient Crete. Old Tamil is one of the classical languages of India and the oldest attested member of the Dravidian languages. The lexicon of the Linear A script appears to be primarily Tamil and to a lesser extent Elamite while the morphology appears to be predominantly Elamite.

As discussed earlier, Professor McAlpin has been the chief proponent of the theory linking Proto-Dravidian with Proto-Elamite. Another relevant clue for the link between Tamil and ancient Elamite is that the indigenous name given to the country of Elam, "Haltamti," can be translated as "The land of the Tamils." The name "Elam," given to it by other countries in the area, means metals, gold, or wealth in Tamil. The main reason that Elam was involved in continuous strife with its

CONCLUSION

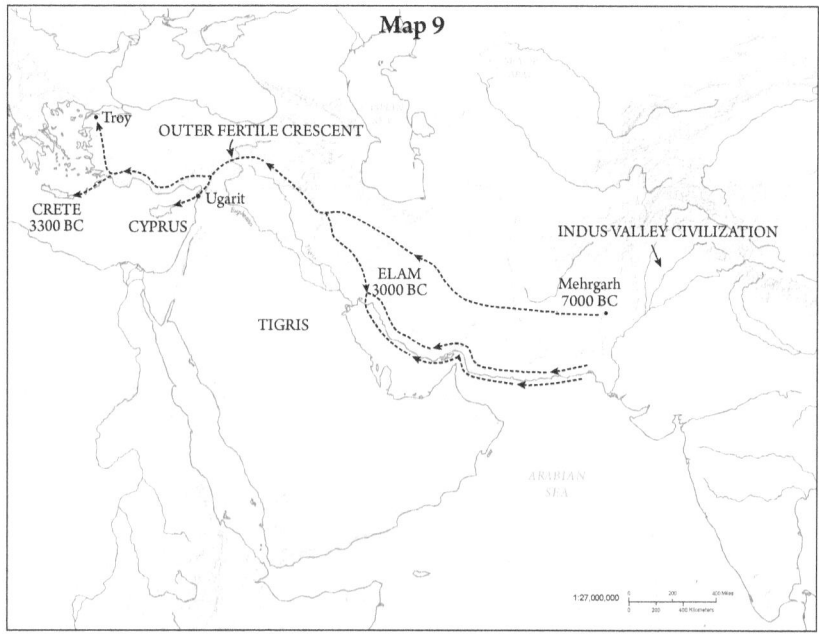

Hypothesized Migrations of the Elamo Dravidians

neighbors was that it was the gateway to the Persian Plateau, which contained metals and other raw materials those countries lacked.

An additional clue for Tamil being the language spoken both by the ancient Cretans as well as by the ancient Lycians is that the indigenous name by which the Lycians called themselves was Termilae ("t" pronounced "th" in Tamil). It has been recorded by the ancient Greek historians that the Lycians originally came from Crete.

The archaeology of Mehrgahr of the Indus Valley Civilization shows that the inhabitants were indigenous to that area from 7000 B.C. Evidence has been presented to show that the language of the Indus Valley Civilization was most probably Dravidian. The geographical, historical, and linguistic evidence already presented also point to a common language spoken in the areas of northern India, the eastern Iranian Plateau, and possibly the southern part of the Central Asian region, a common language that appears to be an archaic form of Tamil. Another link between Crete, Lycia, Elam, and the Indus Valley Civilization is that they were all matriarchal and some were matrilineal societies, which was uncommon for that time. Thus it appears that an ancestral form of the Tamil language, which includes Elamite, was spoken over a wide area in ancient times stretching from the islands of the Aegean to the Indus Valley Civilization of ancient India.

An earlier discussion of the works of Andronov and McAlpin pointed out the relationship between Proto-Dravidian, Brahui, and Proto-Elamite. McAlpin gave evidence to show that Proto-Elamite split off from Proto-Dravidian probably in western Asia around the 5th millennium B.C. Some of these ancient peoples moved westward, probably owing to earthquakes or climatic changes or both.

THE MIGRATIONS OF THE ANCIENT ELAMO-DRAVIDIANS

The great plateau of what we now call central Iran lies east of Mesopotamia, separated from it by the Zagros Mountains. In the central and eastern plateau uninhabitable salt deserts are bounded north and south by ancient trade routes linking east and west. To the north, mountain chains separate the plateau from the Caspian Sea and Central Asia.

The populations of the northern highlands of the plateau shared a culture and ideology, referred to as the "Outer Fertile Crescent" because it overarches the region traditionally known as the Fertile Crescent. In this region during the 3rd millennium B.C. were a number of cities along the piedmont of the Taurus range that are considered to have been culturally Hurrian. It can be hypothesized that peoples speaking an Elamo-Dravidian language settled the same northern region at an earlier time. Some of them probably migrated to Ugarit on the Mediterranean coast where they may have founded a Minoan settlement, as the Cypro-Minoan script indicates, ending up at a still later date in Cyprus. Others may have gone through southern Anatolia on to Crete through the islands of Rhodes and Karpathos, or directly to Crete around 3300 B.C. Still others may have travelled along the coast of Anatolia ending up in pre-Indo-European Troy. This would be the western migratory route of the Elamo-Dravidians.

Still others took a southerly route from the highland area of the Outer Fertile Crescent to end up in Elam.

Routes taken by sea and the southern coast of the plateau from the Indus Valley Civilization (IVC) are trade routes, because the IVC had extensive trade with the Mesopotamian cities as well as Persian Gulf cities, as the Indus seals indicate. The migratory routes of the Elamo-Dravidians are illustrated in Map Eight.

Just as genetic mapping is showing the migration of homo sapiens from the Rift Valley of Africa to the rest of the world, so corroborative evidence for the migratory routes of the Elamo-Dravidians would come from genetic mapping of the regions discussed.

RECIPROCAL INFLUENCE OF THE ELAMO-DRAVIDIANS AND THEIR SURROUNDING CULTURES

Each of the Elamo-Dravidian civilizations influenced the cultures around them in fundamental ways and were in turn influenced by them.

The Mycenaean Greeks of the Mainland were influenced by ancient Crete from 1600 B.C. on, as shown by artifacts in the shaft graves as well as by their later occupation of Crete and the Aegean Islands. They also occupied Cyprus. Historically they had extensive contact with the Lycians. The Doric Greeks, too, occupied Crete and some of the other Aegean islands at a later date. The Ionians Greeks settled on the west coast of Asia Minor, including the ancient Cretan city of Miletus.

The Elamites influenced the Mesopotamian cultures of the time, as well as that of the Persians.

The Indo-Aryans were heavily influenced by the Dravidians.

Minoan Crete influenced the Classical Greeks of the 5th and 4th centuries B.C. in most aspects of their cultural, material, and intellectual lives. The city of Miletus, for example, a likely Minoan settlement on the Ionian Coast, is the birthplace of Greek philosophy. The Minoans started building their first palaces around 2000 B.C, while Classical Greece reached its efflorescence1500 years later in the 5th century B.C.

Greek culture whose underpinnings were those of Minoan Crete, was in some respects a brilliant one. In my opinion, however, it was lacking in a crucial element of a civilized society: human rights and respect for the individual. Slavery was an integral form of their economy just as it was for the Mycenaean Greeks, and Classical Greeks practiced a particularly brutal form. Estimates are that about half the population of ancient Greece were slaves. War was a major source of slaves, and captives could be Greek or non-Greek. During the Peloponnesian War of 431-404 B.C. the Athenians put to death the entire male population of the defiant island of Melos, and enslaved the women and children. Families were broken up when members were sold at the slave markets. Unwanted infants, particularly girls, were exposed to the elements, and, if they did not die, became the slaves of whoever rescued them. Modern archaeology has revealed that conditions in the state-run silver mines of Laurium were nothing short of hellish: slaves, including children, worked 10-hour days in black crawl tunnels, many of them being considered expendable and dying. These mines may have employed as many as 30,000 slaves in the 400s to 300s B.C.

Slavery was paralleled by the devaluation of women. They were considered morally inferior to men and incapable of rational thought. They were segregated in the upper stories of houses, could not go outside the house unaccompanied, and were under the complete control of a male -- either father or husband. Marriage was a contract that was made for a woman in her early teens and the average female died at about age 36. In his funeral oration, Pericles, the Athenian leader declared, "The highest honor for women is to be least talked about by men whether in praise or criticism."

Paradoxically Pericles himself clearly showed the psychological mechanism of "splitting." His long-time companion Aspasia was an intelligent and sophisticated woman whom he treated as an equal, and whom was said to have been influential in his governing decisions. She was reputed to be an hetairai (courtesan), though modern scholars dismiss the charge as the joke of contemporary comic playwrights. Pericles could not marry her because she was non-Athenian, being from Miletus, which had been a Minoan city in ancient times. The Classical Greeks also practiced an institutionalized form of homosexuality and homosexual pedophilia.

There have always, however, been men and women who transcend their culture and their times. One of them was the Greek philosopher Plato, who believed that slavery should be abolished and that women should be accorded equal status.

The Lycians influenced their surrounding cultures by means of their federated democratic structures, which prevented internal conflict, and by their fierce resistance to subjugation. Their constitution was much envied and studied by the classical Greeks who were constantly warring among themselves. The Lycians had a matriarchal and matrilineal system.

The Elamites, too, had a federated system. In addition, they had a system of matrilineal succession, through the "sister's son" by which respect was shown to the woman in that it was her son who became the heir. Governance and administrative functions were left to the men.

The Dravidians appear to have influenced the Indo-Aryans mostly in the areas of their intellectual, philosophical, and religious life. Reciprocally the Indo-Aryans had a highly negative impact on the Dravidians with their rigid caste system and their devaluation of women.

It can be seen that that the neighboring cultures of the ancient Tamils were uncompromisingly patriarchal. Almost all of these neighboring cultures practiced subjugation, with class and caste distinction, as well as slavery and the relegation of women to inferior status. Subjugation applied not only to their treatment of foreign peoples but also to that of their own. Their system has survived over the millennia to this day due to the dominance of their descendants. Certainly it can be said that Western Civilization was founded on the civilizations of ancient Greece and later Rome, with their advanced material and intellectual cultures, but also with a violation of human rights. History over the millennia deals with incessant warfare for dominance and subjugation.

The ancient Tamils ranging from Crete to India provided an alternative model. While having matriarchal systems, they accorded men and women equal status, yet also taking into account the differing roles of men and women. As in the case of the Lycians, they espoused democratic ideals, had federated structures to prevent internal warfare, and were roughly egalitarian in nature. They influenced the Greeks and the Indo-Aryans in the intellectual and religious spheres as well. For example, religious ideas like transmigration and the epiphany of the goddess survived into ancient Greek religion in the form of Orphism and in the Indian religions in the ritual of the Puja.

Ancient Crete had an advanced culture with technological mastery and artistic brilliance. In addition it could be considered to be an advanced civilization in that human rights were respected. There is a hint of slavery in ancient Crete in that the Greek historians allude to captive youths sent as a result of the treaty between Minos and Athens being given as slaves to the victors of the funereal games. The background to this is discussed in the section on the Minoan civilization. Also Herodotus recorded that a son born to a women even from a slave was given citizen status in ancient Lycia. These writings need to be viewed as seen through the prism of the Greeks. They also represent special situations. The treaty between Minos and the Athenians took place as a result of the murder of Minos's son by the Greeks. In the reference to matriarchy in Lycia by Herodotus, the so-called slave could be referring to foreigners workers in Lycia.

The present day Dravidians, including the Tamils, have betrayed the ideals of egalitarianism and human rights. They have instituted a rigid caste system, denigrated women, and have become as oppressive as their northern counterparts in India. In some respects at present, while the West has begun to show increasing tolerant elements of civilization such as secularism, toleration, freedom of thought, and respect for the individual, the Tamils of South India and of other countries have remained in a petrified past. The advanced Tamil cultures that flourished during the 3rd and 2nd millennia of the Bronze Age have remained for the most part unacknowledged and forgotten, "unconscious" so to speak. The ideals that they espoused have throughout the ages been expressed by individuals and groups of individuals but never by large-scale societies as was done by the ancient Tamils.

SELECTED BIBLIOGRAPHY

BACKGROUND AND HISTORICAL SECTION

GENERAL READING

Mallory, J. P. *In Search of the Indo-Europeans.* London: Thames & Hudson, 1996.

AEGEAN, ANATOLIAN, AND EASTERN MEDITERRANEAN REGIONS

Arrian. *The Campaigns of Alexander.* Penguin.

Blegan, C. W. *Troy and the Trojans.* New York: Praeger, 1963.

Bean, G. E. *Lycian Turkey.* London: John Murray, 1989.

de Boer, Jelle Zeilinga, Donald Theodore Sanders, and Robert D. Ballard. *Volcanoes in Human History.* Princeton: Princeton University Press, 2004.

Bryce, T. R. *The Lycians in Literary and Epigraphic Sources,* Vol. 1. Copenhagen: Museum Tusculanum Press, 1986.

Cavanagh, W. G. "A Second Burial Custom?" BICS 25 (1978): 171-2.

Chadwick, J. *The Mycenaean World.* Cambridge: Cambridge University Press, 1976.

Dickinson, Oliver. *The Aegean Bronze Age*. Cambridge: Cambridge University Press, 1994.

Evans, A. J. *The Palace of Minos at Knossos*. Vols. 1-4. London: Macmillan, 1921-1935.

Hagg, R. "Epiphany in Minoan Ritual." BICS 30 (1983): 184-5.

Hallager, E. and M. Vlasakis. "New Tablets from Khania" in J. Driessen and A. Farnoux (eds). *La Crete Mycenienne*. [CH Supplement 30] Paris, 1997.

Herodotus. *The Histories*. New York: Penguin Books.

Homer. *The Iliad*. New York: Anchor Press/Doubleday, 1975.

—, *The Odyssey*. New York: Anchor Press/Doubleday, 1961.

Higgins, R. A. *Minoan and Mycenaean Art*. 2nd ed. London: Thames & Hudson, 1981.

Hood. S. *Arts in Prehistoric Greece*. Harmondsworth, England: Penguin Books, 1978.

—, *The Home of the Heroes: The Aegean before the Greeks*. London: Thames & Hudson 1967.

—, *The Minoans*. London: Thames & Hudson 1971.

Inman, D. L. "Ancient and Modern Harbors." *Proceedings of the 14th Coastal Engineers Conference*.

Kraft, J. C., G. Rapp, I. Kayan, and J. Luce. *Geology* 31 (2003): 163-166.

Nilsson, M. P. *The Minoan Mycenaean Religion*. Cheshire, Conn.: Biblo & Tannen, 1949

Nilsson, M. P. *The Mycenaean Origin of Greek Mythology*. Hong Kong: Forgotten Books, 2007.

Pausanius. *Guide to Greece*, Vols.1-2. New York: Penguin, 1979.

SELECTED BIBLIOGRAPHY

Payne, Annick. *Hieroglyphic Luwian.* Wiesbaden: Otto Harrassowitz, 2004.

Sacks, David. *Encyclopedia of the Ancient Greek World.* New York: Facts on File, 1997.

Sakellarkis, Y., and Efie Sapouna-Sakellarki. "Drama of Death in a Minoan Temple." *National Geographic Magazine,* February 1981.

Schliemann, Heinrich. *Ilios.* New York: Harper, 1881.

Schuchardt, Karl. *Schliemann's Excavations.* London and New York: Macmillan, 1891.

Shelmerdine, Cynthia W., ed. *The Aegean Bronze Age.* Cambridge: Cambridge University Press, 1978.

Strabo: *The Geography.* Vols. 5-6. Cambridge, Mass.: Harvard University Press.

Sinkin, Tom, Lee Siebert, and Kimberly Paul. *Volcanoes of the World.* Geoscience Press, 2011

Taylour, Lord William. *The Mycenaeans.* 2nd ed. London: Thames & Hudson, 1983.

Thucidides. *The Peloponnesian War.* Baltimore: Penguin Books, 1954.

Trzaskomo, Stephen, R., Scott Smith, and Stephen Brunet, eds. *Anthology of Classical Myth.* Indianapolis/Cambridge: Hackett Publishing Company, 1984.

Vassos, Karageorghis. *Cyprus: From the Stone Age to the Romans.* London: Thames & Hudson, 1982.

Ventris, M. and J. Chadwick. *Documents in Mycenaean Greek.* Cambridge: Cambridge University Press, 1956.

ELAM

Amiet, P. *Elam*. Auvers-sur-Oise, France: 1966.

Bretjes, Buchard. *The History of Elam and Achaemenid Persia*. In Sasson, Jack M., ed., *Civilizations of the Ancient Near East*. New York: Scribner, 1995.

Carter, Elizabeth and Matthew W. Stolper. *Elam, Surveys of Political History and Archaeology*. Berkeley: University of California Press, 1984.

Fisher, W.B., ed. *Cambridge History of Iran. Vol. 1. The Land of Iran*. Cambridge: Cambridge University Press, 1968.

Hallock, R. T. *Persepolis Fortification Tablets*. Chicago: University of Chicago Press, 1969.

Vallat, Francois. *Susa and Susiana. Second Millennium Iran*. In Sasson, Jack M., ed. *Civilizations of the Ancient Near East*. New York: Scribner, 1995.

ANCIENT INDIA AND THE INDUS VALLEY CIVILIZATION

Allchin, B. and R. Allchin. *The Rise of Civilization in India and Pakistan*. Cambridge: Cambridge University Press, 1982.

Avati, Burjar. *India: the Ancient Past*. London: Routledge, 2007.

Kenoyer, J. M. *Ancient Cities of the Indus Valley Civilization*. Oxford: Oxford University Press, 1998.

Wheeler, Sir Mortimer. *The Indus Civilization*. Cambridge University Press. 1962.

Marshall, J. *Mohenjo-Daro and the Indus Civilization*. New Delhi: Asian Educational Services, 1996.

SELECTED BIBLIOGRAPHY

Basham, A. L. *The Wonder that was India*. London: Sidgwick & Jackson, 1954

Basham, A. L. *History and Doctrines of the Ajivikas*. London, 1957.

Couze, E. *A Short History of Buddhism*. Oxford: One World, 1993.

Dani, A. H. *The Historic City of Taxila*. Paris, Unesco, 1986.

Davids, T. W. Rhys. *Buddhism: Its History and Literature*. 2nd ed. London, 1926.

Stevenson, Sinclair. *The Heart of Jainism*. Forgotten Books, 1911.

Bhandarkar, R. G. *Vaishnavism, Saivism, and Minor Religious Sects*. Strasburg, 1913.

Shashtri, H. P. *The Ramayana of Valmiki*. 3 vols. London, 1952-59.

Roy, P. C. *The Mahabharata,* 2nd ed. 11 vols. Bharata Press: Calcutta, 1914-55.

Griffith, R. T. H. *Hinduism: The Rig Veda*. New York: Quality Paperback Book Club, 1992.

Whitney, W. D. and C. R. Lanman. *The Artharva Veda*. 2 vols. Cambridge, Mass.: Harvard University, 1905.

Eggeling, J. *The Satapatha Brahmana*. 5 vols. Oxford: Clarenden Press, 1885-1900.

Roebuck V. *The Upanishads*. New York: Penguin Books, 2003.

Rocher, L. *The Puranas*. Wiesbaden: Otto Harrassowitz, 1986.

Sharma, J. P. *Republics of Ancient India*. Leiden: E. J. Brill. 1968.

SELECTED BIBLIOGRAPHY

LANGUAGE SECTION

THE LINEAR B SCRIPT

Chadwick, John. *Linear B and Related Scripts: Reading the Past*. London: British Museum, 1987.

Chadwick, John. *The Mycenaean World*. Cambridge: Cambridge University Press, 1976.

Chadwick, John. *The Decipherment of Linear B*. Cambridge: Cambridge University Press, 1958.

Hallager, E. and M. Vlasaki. "New Linear B Tablets from Khania." *Bulletin De correspondence Hellenique*. Supplement No. 30 (1997): 169 - 174.

Robinson, Andrew. *Lost Languages*. New York: McGraw Hill, 2002.

Ventris, Michael and John Chadwick. *Documents in Mycenaean Greek*. Cambridge: Cambridge University Press, 1973.

THE LINEAR A SCRIPT

Bennett, E. L., Jr. "Fractional Quantities in Minoan Bookkeeping." *American Journal of Archaeology* 54 (1950): 204-222.

—, "The three R's of the Linear A and Linear B Writing System." *Semiotica* 122 (1998): 139-163.

SELECTED BIBLIOGRAPHY

Brice, W. C. *Inscriptions in the Minoan Linear Script of Class A*. Oxford: University Press, 1961.

—, "A comparison of the Account Tablets of Susa in the ProtoElamite Script with those of Hagia Triada in Linear A," *Kadmos* 2 (1963): 28-34.

—, "The Structure of Linear A with some Proto-Elamite and Proto-Indic Comparisons." *Europa, Festschrift fur Ernst Grumach* (W. C. Brice, ed.). Berlin, 1967.

Evans, A. J. *Scripta Minoa 1*. Oxford: Clarenden Press, 1909.

Heubeck, A. "Linear B und das Agäische Substrat." *Minos* 5 (1957): 149-153.

Payne, Annick. *Hieroglyphic Luwian*. Wiesbaden: Otto Harrassowitz, 2010.

Pope, G. U. *A Handbook of the Tamil Language*. New Deli: Asian Educational Services, 1979.

Packard, David, W. *Minoan Linear A*. Berkeley: University of California Press, 1974.

Pugliese, Carratelli, G. "Le epigrafi di Hagia Triada in Lineare A." (Supplement to Minos) Salamanca, 1963.

Raison, J. and M. Pope. *Index du Lineaire A*. Rome, 1971.

Finkelberg, M. "The Language of Linear A: Greek, Semitic, or Anatolian?" *The Journal of Indo-European Studies*, Monograph 38, Washington, D. C., 2001.

Duhoux, Y. "da-ma-te = Demeter? Sur la langue du lineaire A" *Minos* 29-30 (1994-95): 289-294.

Godart, L. and J. P. Olivier. *Recueil des Inscriptions en Lineaire A*. Vols. 1 - 5. Paris, 1976 - 1983

Raison, J. and M. Pope. *Corpus transnumere du Lineaire A*. Louvain, 1980.

Robinson, Andrew. *Lost Languages*. New York: McGraw Hill, 2002

THE LYCIAN SCRIPT AND LANGUAGES

Heubeck, Alfred. "Konsonatische Gemminaten im lykishen Wortanlaut." *Zeitschrift fur Verleischende Sprachforschung Zeitschrift*. 98 (1985): 36-46.

Melchert, H, Craig. "Lycian." In *Encyclopedia of the World's Ancient Languages*. Roger Woodward, ed. Cambridge: Cambridge University Press, 2005.

------, *Lycian Lexicon* (2nd fully revised edition). Chapel Hill: Self Published, 1993.

Bryce, T. *The Lycians in Literary and Epigraphic Sources*. Copenhagen: Museum Tusculaneum Press, 1986.

Kalinka, E. *Tituli Lyciae, Lingua Lycia Conscript*. Vienna Hoelder-Pichler-Tempsky, 1901.

Metzger, Henri et al. "La stele Trilingue." *Fouille de Xanthos*. Vol. 1. Paris: Klincksieck, M. 1979.

THE ELAMITE SCRIPTS AND LANGUAGES

Yarshater, Ehsan, ed. *Encyclopedia Iranica*.

Englund, R. "The Proto-Elamite script." In *World's Writing Systems*. Daniels, P and W. Bright, eds. Oxford: Oxford University Press, 1996.

Grillot-Susini, F. and C. Roche. *Elements de Grammaire Elamite*. Paris; Editions Recherche sur les Civilisations, 1987.

SELECTED BIBLIOGRAPHY

Hallock, R. Persepolis Fortification Tablets. Oriental Institute Publications. 92. Chicago: University of Chicago Press, 1969.

Walther Hinz and Heidemarie Koch. *Elamisches Worterbuch*. Archaologissche Mitteilungen aus Iran, 1987.

Salvini, M. "Elam iv. Linear Elamite." *Encyclopedia Iranica*, Vol. 8. Yarshater, Ehsan, ed.

Stolper, Matthew W. "Elamite." In *Cambridge Encyclopedia of the World's Ancient Languages*. Roger D. Woodward, ed. 2008.

PROTO-ELAMO-DRAVIDIAN, PROTO DRAVIDIAN, OLD TAMIL

Caldwell, R. *A Comparative Grammar of the Dravidian or South- Indian Family of Languages*. 2nd ed. University of Madras, Madras, 1875.

Emeneau, M. B. *Collected Papers: Dravidian Linguistics, Ethnology and Folktales*. Annamalainagar, India: Annamalai University Press, 1967.

McAlpin, David W. *Proto-Elamo-Dravidian: The evidence and its implications*. Transactions of the American Philosophical society, Vol. 71 Part 1.

Pope, G. U. *A Handbook of the Tamil language*. New Delhi: Asian Educational Services, 1979.

Schiffman, H. *A Grammar of Spoken Tamil*. Madras: Christian Literature Society, 1979.

Steever, Sanford, B. "Tamil and the Dravidian Languages." In *The World's Major Languages*. Bernard, Comrie, ed.

Steever, Stanford, B. "Old Tamil." In *Cambridge Encyclopedia of the World's Ancient Languages*. Woodward, Roger D., ed., 2008.

INDUS SCRIPT

Mahadevan, Iravatham. "Aryan or Dravidian or Neither? A Study of Recent Attempts to Decipher the Indus Script." *EJVS* Vol. 8, issue 1, 2008.

Parpola, Asko. *Deciphering the Indus Script*. Cambridge: Cambridge University Press, 1994.

THE CYPRIOT SCRIPTS

Chadwick, John. *Linear B and Related Scripts*. University of California Press, 1987.

Masson, O. *Les Inscriptions Chypriotes Syllabique*. Paris, 2nd ed., 1983.

ONLINE RESOURCES

Ancient Scripts.com

Omniglot: Writing Systems & Languages of the World.
http://www.omniglot.com/writing

Mnamon: Antiche Scritture del Meditteraneo.

Rutter, J. B. "The Prehistoric Archaeology of the Aegean." http://projectsx.dartmouth.edu/history/bronze_age/

Younger, J. G., ed.
http://people.ku.edu/~jyounger/LinearA/

ABBREVIATIONS

BICS – *Bulletin of the Institute of Classical Studies*

EJVS – *Electronic Journal of Vedic Studies*

INDEX

Achilles, 8
Aegean Bronze Age, 1, 7, 16, 21, 26, 41
Aeolic islands, 12
Agamemnon, 8, 48
Ajivikas, 88
Akkadian language, 1, 106
Arcadia, 11, 25, 123
Archanes, 28
Arcadio-Cypriot subgroup of the Greek
  Language, 11, 25, 63, 123
Arrian, 89
Artemis, 43
Aryan Migration into India, 78–94
  Settlement in the Punjab, 81
  Settlement in the Madhyadesha, 84
  Expansion Along the Gangetic Basin, 85
  Expansion South, 92
Aryan Religion
  Vedic Hinduism, 82
  Hinduism, 91, 92
Arzawa, 99
Asia Minor, 7, 12, 16, 24, 26, 42, 43, 50, 51
Atlantis Legend, 18
Athena, 40
Aphrodite, 40
Avestan, 79, 80, 81, 82

Banti, Luisa, 46
Bhagavad Gita, 84
Bellerphon, 13
Bennet, Emmett, 129, 130, 133
Blegen, Carl, 59, 129
Bolan pass, 73, 79
Brahmans, 83, 85, 89, 93
Brahui, 114, 118, 178
Buddha, 88
Bull Leaping Sport, 35, 36, 41

Caria, 55, 98
Carian language, 98, 104
Carian script, 101
Caste, 80, 83–84, 88, 93, 94
Cavanagh, W.G., 50
Chadwick, John, 1, 25, 42, 61, 129, 157
Champollion, Jean-Francois, 129
Chronology of Ancient Crete, 10
  Evans' classification, 14,
  Platons classification, 14,
  Proposed modified chronology, 20
Cocolas, 52.
Crete, Bronze Age, 1, 2, 9, 15, 18, 19, 24, 25, 26,
  51
Cyclades, 50
Cyprus script, 97
Cypro-Minoan script, 11, 62, 122, 123, 179
Cypriot syllabary, 63, 101, 121, 122, 123, 125, 130,
  133, 137
Cyprus, 11, 24, 29, 63
  History, 62–63

Daidolos, 18, 52
Dark Age of ancient Greece, 10, 14, 61
Dating methods in archaeology, 10
Decipherment of the Linear A script, 158–175
Decipherment of the Linear B script, 97,
  129–138
Demeter, 41, 42, 44
Democratic Lycian Federation, 56
Democritus, 87
Diktean or Psychro cave, 37
Diodorus Siculus, 41, 89, 141
Diomedes, 12
Dionysius, 44,
Dodecanese, 25, 50
Dorian invasion, 11

195

CIVILIZATIONS OF THE UNCONSCIOUS

Doric style capitals, 24
Dove Shrine Deposit, 38, 40
Dravidians, 78, 85, 93, 113

Egypt, 29, 33
Egyptian texts, 56, 99
Eileithiya, 43
Elam, 64–70
   Historical and language Periods, 65–68
   Connections to the Indus valley and
     Central Asia, 70–71
   Language and scripts, 106–112
   Federation, 68, 182
   Matriarchy and Matrilineality, 68–70
Elamo-Dravidian migrations, 178
Elamo-Dravidian Languages, 2, 179
   Proto-Elamo-Dravidian, 113
   Proto Dravidian, 114, 176
   Dravidian, 114, 117, 119
Elamite Script, 97, 106
   Proto-Elamite, 107, 108
   Linear Elamite, 108
   Cuneiform Elamite, 108
Eleusian Mysteries, 44
Elysion, 44
Engyum, 52
Ephorus, 55, 98
Epirus, 25
Etruscans, 53, 126
Eteo-Cypriot Language, 123, 125
Eteo-Cretan Language, 141
Eteocretans, 53
Evans, Sir Arthur, 9,
Evans' classification, 14

Federalist papers, 67–68
Federated states of Elam, 68
Fractiolnal burial rite, 80
Frescoes, Cretan, 31, 33

Gana Sanghas, 89
Ghagger Hakra River, 73, 77, 81, 82
Ghandara Grave Culture, 80
Ghandi, 91
Glaucus, 13
Godart, Louis, and Olivier, Jean-Pierre, 149
Greeks
   Classical, 8, 180
   Dorian, 11, 19, 25, 53, 180
   Ionian, 11, 180
   Macedonian, 63
   Mycenaean, 2, 8, 11, 19, 21, 63, 123, 108, 180
Greek pantheon, 41, 42

Greek language, 1
Greek myths and legends, 14
Grey Ware ceramics, 80

Hagia Triada, 11, 30, 45, 46
   Sarcophagus, 46
   Steatite vases, 46
Halberr, Fredrico, 45
Hamilton, Alexander, 58
Harappans, 85
Hector, 8, 61
Hellenic Volcanic Arc, 18
Helen of Troy, 8, 60
Helmand River, 79, 81
Herodotus, 18, 52, 55, 58, 183
Hieroglyphic, Script, 9, 26, 29, 139, 140
Historicity of the ancient Greek writings, 10
Hittite language, 1
Hittites, 42, 56, 78
Hittite texts 1, 56, 98
Homer, 7, 12, 53
Homeric epics, 10, 12
Horns of Consecration, 30, 38, 70
Hrozny, Bedric, 129
Hypothesized Linear A syllabary, 142–150

Iasos, 50, 51
Idalion Tablet, 123
Idomeneus, 19
Iliad, The, 7, 8, 12, 19, 52, 59, 61, 84, 129
Indian Caste System, 84, 94
Indian Religion
   Buddhism, 88, 90, 93
   Cosmogonic theories, 87
   Hinduism, 91–93
   Jainism, 88, 91
   Mysticism and Asceticism, 86
Indic language, 1
Indus Valley Civilization, 73, 77
   Harappan Phases, 74–77
   Regional cultures, 77
   Religion, 76
   Seals, 119
   numerical system, 120
Indus script, 75, 97, 117, 119
Insusinak, Puzur, 108
Interconnections between Elam and the IVC, 71
Iphigenia, 48
Iolkos, 21
Ionia, 51
Isopata ring, 41.
Iyengar, Srinivasan, 94

INDEX

Kamares ware, 29, 37, 47
Karma, 86, 91
Kassites, 78
Kato Zakros, palace of, 28
Keos, 50
Khania, 19, 53
Khyber pass, 78
Knidos, 50
Knossos, 9
    Palace, 9, 28, 29–31
Kober, Alice, 130, 132, 152
Kraft and Luce, 12,
Kutik-in-Shusinak, 67
Kythera, 24, 29, 60, 139

Laconia, 50
Language and scripts of ancient Lycia and Caria, 98–105
Language and scripts of ancient Elam, 106–112
Languages and scripts of ancient Cyprus, 122–127
Letoon Trilingual Stele, 56, 99
Levant, 26
Linear A Script, 2, 9, 26, 29, 97, 139, 141
    Decipherment, 139–175
    Transaction signs, 158
    Numerical and metrical system, 159
    Linear B logograms, 163–164
    Classification of the Linear A tablets, 164–171.
    Religious Inscriptions, 171–174
Linear A tablets, 2, 11, 43, 45
Linear B script, 9, 26, 97, 123, 141
    Bennetts Classification, 130
    Kobers Identification, 130
    Decipherment of the Linear B script, 131–133
    Numerical and metrical system, 135
    Linear B logograms, 137
    Classification of the Linear B tablets, 133–134
    Spelling conventions, 135–137
Linear B tablets, 19, 20, 21, 45
Linear B tablet, Tn 316, 25, 48
Luwian language, 1, 61, 99, 100
Lycians, 55, 99, 98, 142, 182
Lycian history, 55–58
Lycian language, 98–104
Lycian League, 57
Lycian Scripts, 102
Lycurgus, 51

Madison, James, 58

Mahabharata, 84, 85, 86, 93
Mahadevan, 120
Mahavira, 90
Mallia, palace of, 28
Marshall, Sir John, 76, 118
Matrilineal succession, 68
McAlpin, David, 2, 106, 113, 118, 176
Megasthenes, 89
Mehrgahr, 73, 177
Melchart, Professor Craig, 99
Melos, 29
Menelaos, 8
Middle Helladic Period, 24
Miletus, 50, 51, 55, 98, 180
Minoa, 41
Minoan Civilization, 9, 10,
    Architecture, 33
    Cannibalism, 49–50
    Chronology, 26–31
    Dorian occupation, 53
    Frescoes, 31, 33
    Funerary and burial rites, 45
    Human sacrifice, 47–49
    Palaces,
        Kato Zakros, 28
        Knossos, 9, 28, 29–31
        Mallia, 28
        Phaistos, 23, 28, 30
    Pottery, 33–35
    Metal work and Jewellry, 35
    Religion, 37
        Caves, 37
            Arkolochari Cave, 37
            Cave of Eleithiya, 37, 43
            Diktean or Psychro Cave, 37
            Idean Cave, 37
            Kamares Cave, 37
        Idean Cave, 37
        Peak Sanctuaries, 38
        Domestic shrines, 38
        Outdoor shrines, 38
        Cultic symbols, 38
Minos, 18, 51, 51, 52, 55, 99, 120, 183
Minotaur, 52
Mittani, 78
Mochlos, 27
Mount Juktas, 28
Mount Ida, 28, 33
Mount Dikte, 37
Mycenae, 8, 9, 19, 21
Mycenaean citadel, 21, 24
Mycenaean Civilization, 9, 10, 21–25
Mycenaean occupation of Crete, 19, 45

CIVILIZATIONS OF THE UNCONSCIOUS

Mylonas, 23
Myrtos, 27

Naram-Sin, Treaty of, 66, 69
Neolithic Age, 7, 27, 73
Neolithic people, 27, 141
Nile Delta, 18
Nilsson, Martin, P., 42
Nirou Khani, 29
Non-Rigvedic Aryans, 79, 80

Odyssey, The, 8, 37, 43, 44, 59, 84
Odysseus, 8, 53
Orchemenos, 21
Orphism, 44–45

Palmer, L.R., 20
Pamphylia, 11, 123
Pantheon of Classical Greece, 41
Papademetriou, 23
Papyrus, 11
Parian Marble, 51, 52, 99
Paris, 8
Paros, 50
Parpola, Asko, 120
Pausanius, 8, 42
Pelasgians, 42
Peloponnese, 25, 50, 123
Pericles, 181
Persephone, 44
Persian Plateau Settlements
   Shar-I Sokhata, 71
     Konar Sanda, 71
     Shadad, 71
Phaistos Disc, 29, 139, 140
Phaistos tablet, 140
Pharos, 28
Phylokapi, 29, 50
Pillar crypt, 18
Plato, 16
Polochni, 60
Poseidon, 45
Pylos, 19, 21, 24, 25

Ramayana, 84, 93
Rawlinson, Henry, 129
Rhodes, 29, 50, 179
Rigveda, 79, 81, 82, 85, 86, 117, 119
Rigvedic Aryans, 79
Rulers of Crete, 50
Rufus Quintus Curtius, 89

Sakellarakis, Y., 47

Sanskrit, 78, 80
Sapouna-Sakellaraki, E., 47
Sarasvati river, 81
Schliemann, Heinrich, 7, 8, 9, 59
Semitic languages, 1, 142
Shaft Graves, 21
Shilkhakha, 69
Snake Goddesses, 29, 38
Sparta, 51
Stolper, Matthew, 101
Strabo's Geographica, 12
Sumerian kingdom, 7, 66, 16
Swat valley, 78, 79, 80
Syria, 29

Tamils, 56, 64, 94, 106, 115, 175, 176, 178, 183, 184
Tamil Alphabet, 142–145
Thebes, 19, 21
The Little Palace, 29
The Royal Villa, 29
The House of The Frescoes, 29
Thera, 13, 16, 18, 24, 28, 29, 50
Tholos tombs, 23, 29
Tiryns, 8
Tomb of Clytemnestra, 23
Transmigration, 45, 86
Treasury of Atreus, 23, 24
Trojan war, 11, 18, 52, 63
Troy, 7, 8, 9, 12, 19, 52, 59–61
   The nine levels 59–60
   Seal with Luwian writing, 61

Ugarit, 122
Ugaritic texts, 56

Vallat, 106
Vapheio, Cups, 23, 29, 35, 37
Vasiliki, 27
Vedas, 41, 81, 82, 84, 85, 86, 89, 92
Vedic Commentaries
   Brahmanas, 83, 85, 86, 92
   Aranyakas, 85, 86
   Upanishads, 85, 86, 87
Vedic Hinduism, 76, 82, 84, 91, 92, 93
   Vaishnava, 92
   Shaiva, 92
   Shakti, 92
Ventris, Michael, 25, 41, 61, 123, 129, 130, 131–138, 123, 130
131, 132, 152
Vellalars, 93
Vyasa, 86, 94

INDEX

Wall, Musgrave and Warren, 49
Wanax, 21

Xanthos Obelisk, 100

Zarathustra, 81
Zeus, 41, 51, 81, 82